Down Ballot

Down Ballot

How a Local Campaign Became a National Referendum on Abortion

PATRICK WOHL

3 FIELDS BOOKS
An imprint of the University of Illinois Press

3 Fields Books is an imprint of the
University of Illinois Press.

Library of Congress Cataloging-in-Publication Data

Names: Wohl, Patrick, 1994– author.
Title: Down ballot : how a local campaign became a national
    referendum on abortion / Patrick Wohl.
Description: Urbana : University of Illinois Press, [2024] |
    Includes bibliographical references and index.
Identifiers: LCCN 2023012603 (print) | LCCN 2023012604
    (ebook) | ISBN 9780252045479 (cloth) | ISBN
    9780252087585 (paperback) | ISBN 9780252055096
    (ebook)
Subjects: LCSH: Illinois. General Assembly. House of
    Representatives—Elections, 1990. | Contested elections—
    Illinois. | Pullen, Penny. | Mulligan, Rosemary, 1941–2014
    | Republican Party (Ill.) | Abortion—Political aspects—
    United States. | Illinois—Politics and government—1951–
Classification: LCC JK5793 1990 .W65 2024 (print) | LCC
    JK5793 1990 (ebook) | DDC 324.6/509773—dc23/
    eng/20230909
LC record available athttps://lccn.loc.gov/2023012603
LC ebook record available at https://lccn.loc.gov/2023012604

Both sides of the abortion debate are studying the results of a significant primary election in Illinois, where the deciding issue appears to have been abortion.

Diane Sawyer, *ABC News*, March 21, 1990

Contents

Acknowledgments

My first thanks go out to all the people who were kind enough to lend me their time and talk about what they remember from these two political campaigns. After more than thirty years, I was amazed at each interviewee's ability to dig up old memories, some of which proved painful even with time. I'd like to thank in particular Burt Odelson, Mary Ann Irvine, Cal Skinner, Matt Bonaguidi, Diddy Blythe, Francis Barth, Steve Granzyk, and Terry Cosgrove for being incredible sources of knowledge. Thank you to Penny Pullen for answering my questions. I'd also like to thank Barbara Scharringhausen, Ellen Yearwood, Gary Gale, Jane West, John Atkinson, Ken South, Kristine Gebbie, Madeline Doubek, Mat Delort, Mike O'Malley, Peggy DuFour, Ralph Rivera, Sandy Deines, Tim Schmitz, and Todd Wessell for their time. This book would also not be possible without the work of dozens of reporters who covered the Pullen-Mulligan race back in 1990 and 1992, and I'm indebted to their work.

A special thanks to my agent, Leslie York, for taking a chance on me. Your edits and counsel were invaluable, and I absolutely couldn't have done this without all the hard work you put into making the manuscript much smoother and more interesting.

To Martha Bayne and the whole team at the University of Illinois Press for agreeing to take on this project, I so appreciate the great work you all do. There are tons of fascinating stories about Illinois politics just waiting to be told, and you all are the tip of the spear.

A final thanks to all of those who put in extra hours reading (very) rough drafts. These include Lisa Francis and Ben Tracy. And, of course, a special thanks to Chris Chaffee for his unwavering support over the past two years.

Down Ballot

Introduction

David Boies walked onto the famed set of *Meet the Press* in December of 2000 and readied himself for what he expected to be a contentious interview. Boies, one of the country's most well-known attorneys, had recently gained even more notoriety when Vice President Al Gore asked him to lead his legal team to argue for a recount in the state of Florida the month before. The team was preparing to file their legal brief before the United States Supreme Court in the case of *Bush v. Gore*, and Boies was doing a full-court press in the media to complement their effort.

After host Tim Russert pressed the vice president's attorney on their legal strategy and how Boies felt about the case, he ended with a pointed question. "So you're confident the Florida bar will take no action?" Russert asked, alluding to an ethics accusation recently filed against him. Republican lawyers had accused him of falsifying an affidavit to support the Gore team's argument that so-called "dimpled chads" that appeared to be votes for the vice president should be counted for Gore. Voters in a number of counties had experienced trouble using a stylus to punch a full hole through their ballots, and the legal team wanted the canvassing boards conducting a recount to consider the *intent* of the voter, not just the numbers the machines reported out. Boies, a slender man dressed in a plain blue suit, grinned as he gave his unequivocal response. "I'm very confident of that," he said, ending the interview.[1]

Just a few weeks earlier, the Gore legal team had been on the hunt for a case that would support their argument that those dimpled ballots should be counted. With just a few hundred votes separating the two candidates, the eyes of the world were now on these attorneys to see just how the 2000 presidential election would be resolved, and they needed every bit of legal ammunition they could get. Not an election lawyer by trade, Boies had previously led important cases like the federal government's antitrust action in *United States v. Microsoft* and was hired earlier that year to defend the music-sharing website Napster in a make-or-break lawsuit. Still, nothing compared to the intense scrutiny he was currently facing.

Both the Gore and Bush teams were in uncharted territory legally. Election law is a niche field, and there are few cases on recount issues, let alone ones as specific as how to judge the intent of a voter. So when searching for a case to support their proposition, the Gore lawyers were delighted to come across an article in the *Chicago Tribune* discussing an election decided by the Illinois Supreme Court in 1990 that shared many similarities with the issues now being debated in Florida. According to the *Tribune*, Illinois's highest court had ordered "dimpled chads" be counted in a case called *Pullen v. Mulligan*. The precedent couldn't bind the Florida canvassing boards to follow an Illinois standard, but it provided a persuasive argument for why they should anyway.

Without delay, the Gore team tracked down the Chicago attorney who worked on the case a decade earlier. Mike Lavelle was known as the dean of Illinois election lawyers. A former marine and native of Ireland, Lavelle was one of the most respected members of his field and known for his thoroughness and quick recall of the idiosyncrasies of state election law. An avid Chicago Cubs fan, he wore black, thick-rimmed glasses and had a receding hairline. Lavelle wrote many of the rules at issue in the *Pullen v. Mulligan* case, having served on the state and city of Chicago election boards in their infancy.[2] He was woken up at 11 p.m. with a surprising and pressing ask. On the other end of the line, one of Gore's attorneys explained that they saw the *Tribune* story and wondered if he would sign an affidavit affirming what was held in the *Pullen* case. After then speaking with Boies, who further assured him how valuable an affidavit would be, Lavelle agreed. The next morning, Lavelle made some changes to the draft text provided by the Gore team and faxed it back to them in Florida.[3]

The following day, Lavelle realized he had misremembered some of the Illinois Supreme Court's holdings. The court hadn't actually ruled that dimpled chads should be counted in all cases but said they should be counted if the intent of the voter could be ascertained. It was a crucial detail the team had unwittingly left out of the affidavit. In some ways, the Illinois court's holding *hurt* Democrats' legal argument in Florida. Lavelle decided to flag it for the Gore team. "We're fucked," said one of the lawyers upon hearing the news.[4] With attention magnifying every move the team made, they knew it wouldn't slip by their counterparts working for Texas governor George W.

Bush. Indeed, within a few days, a complaint was filed against Boies with the Florida bar accusing him of lying. It was mostly a bogus claim given Boies had no knowledge that any information in the affidavit was false; he was merely putting forth what the article in the *Tribune* erroneously reported and Lavelle had inaccurately confirmed. Still, the media made a stink about it anyway. "Boies Will Be Boies!" crowed a headline in the *New York Post*.[5]

The *Pullen* case became a central point of disagreement between the Bush and the Gore legal teams. One side asserted it meant dimpled chads should be counted while the other insisted it stood for exactly the opposite notion. In fact, Lavelle's opposing counsel on the *Pullen* case in 1990, Illinois attorney Burt Odelson, had even been aiding the Bush team in Florida. Odelson had received a similar call from Governor Bush's campaign chairman Don Evans, and he eventually flew down to Florida to assist with arguments before some of the county canvassing boards. The two friends found themselves again on opposite teams advocating for the same things they'd fought over ten years prior.

As recounts went forward across the state of Florida, each canvassing board began adhering to a different standard based on these arguments. This meant the recount process varied by county, which would eventually be the reason the United States Supreme Court cited for ruling in Bush's favor. The disagreement around the *Pullen* case would become one of the dominos in a long chain of events that would eventually determine who ascended to the presidency.

During the Florida recount, the national media took a new look at the Illinois case, interested in the mechanics of the court's holding. But what many missed in focusing on the legal aspects of *Pullen v. Mulligan* was the story surrounding the actual election ten years earlier. The case involved a recount battle from a state legislative race in suburban Chicago during the March 1990 GOP primary.

A Republican primary in a sleepy suburban district outside Chicago might not sound very interesting, but the campaign had been a media circus of its own at the time. It was a state legislative campaign that found itself in the spotlight as a national proxy war on the issue of abortion. It was a legal battle that would eventually be cited as precedent in the most important election case of our country's history. And it was a story that illustrates the behind-the-scenes machinations of state and local politics that is often overlooked.

Penny Pullen was a longtime conservative leader in the Illinois House. Well-known in Republican circles for her appointments to several commissions by Presidents Ronald Reagan and George H. W. Bush, her biggest devotion was to the cause of restricting abortion. Her strong views on the issue would eventually make her a national target following a Supreme Court decision that reenergized prochoice activists in 1989. Her primary challenger, Rosemary Mulligan, was a single mother, a paralegal, and a staunch prochoice advocate. Mulligan faced many obstacles in her life, but she would find success in her eventual career in politics.

Neither Rosemary Mulligan nor Penny Pullen is a household name today, nor are their raucous political battles remembered in the annals of American political history. Despite this, their story is emblematic of the important work performed by state legislators across the country each year. Much of this work, because it lacks the glamour of national politics, goes entirely unnoticed. Voter turnout in local elections is almost always dwarfed by that in the larger, seemingly more important campaigns. Less money is spent on local races and most candidates don't have the resources to put up flashy TV ads or full-scale field operations. Many state legislators have little to no staff once elected. Yet most of the lawmaking that actually affects Americans' day-to-day lives happens in state capitals, not in Washington.

There are thousands of books, movies, and TV series about presidential campaigns. Stories abound of high-profile Senate races and of campaigns for governor. But very few accounts exist of the campaigns down ballot. This is one of those stories.

On average, state legislatures introduce twenty-three times as many bills as the U.S. Congress annually, close to 130,000 bills each year.[6] Today, a list of our country's most contentious issues could easily be confused for the agenda of a state legislature. Religious liberty or freedom *from* religion. Voting rights or voter ID. The freedom to carry or stricter gun control. Protecting women in sports or protecting the rights of transgender athletes. And yes, abortion. If you look close enough, there is a Rosemary Mulligan and a Penny Pullen advocating passionately for either side of these issues in every state across the country. They're watching carefully. The only question is: Who's watching them?

• • •

Newspapers throughout Illinois carried this advertisement billing the Rev. Jerry Falwell, Phyllis Schlafly, and Penny Pullen as key figures opposing state ratification of the Equal Rights Amendment in the leadup to a rally in May of 1980. Photo Credit: Moral Majority

1

Amendment XXVII

My opponent says a woman's place is in the home.
But my husband replies that a woman's place is in the
House—the United States House of Representatives.

When Penny Pullen first decided to run for state representative, no one mentioned Molotov cocktails. So after receiving news that an improvised explosive device had been thrown at her home, Pullen was beyond relieved to hear it had fizzled out in a bed of flowers near a basement window. After conferring with law enforcement, Pullen and her parents decided not to file a police report; they were better off not drawing more attention to the matter.[1]

The incident was one with which Pullen was becoming all too familiar. In the dead of night on two other occasions, the windows of her suburban legislative office were shattered by orange-sized rocks. When Pullen went to open her car door in another instance, she found a dead frog placed neatly on the passenger's seat. The car window had been left slightly cracked open, but Pullen had a hard time attributing the incident to mother nature.[2] And while she didn't pay much attention to these intimidation tactics, they continued nonetheless.

Early one morning at precisely 3:15 a.m., the phone rang in Pullen's Springfield apartment not far from the state capitol building. In the darkness, she frantically woke to answer the call. But on the other end of the line, Pullen was greeted with silence. "Hello?" she asked. Hearing no one, she hung up. The caller was unlisted, and very few people had the number to her apartment in Illinois's capital city other than some close friends and family.[3] Needless to say, falling back to sleep after this proved challenging.

It was the summer of 1980 and the Illinois General Assembly was in the midst of debating ratification of the Equal Rights Amendment. Despite the innocuous-sounding name, two opposing sides were locked in a stalemate that had been zealously raging ever since the idea was first sent to the states by Congress for approval. Of all places, the main battle over the proposed Twenty-seventh Amendment to the United States Constitution was being waged in Springfield, Illinois.

Just the day before, one of Pullen's fellow legislators rose to challenge other members of the Illinois House of Representatives who were opposing ratification. A supporter of the ERA, this particular legislator was angry. For years, pro-ERA forces had sought to pass an amendment to the Constitution that they believed would right the wrongs of history and bring legal equality to the sexes once and for all. She was dumbfounded why men—and women like Pullen—couldn't bring themselves to support what she viewed as a necessary, inoffensive amendment to one of America's founding documents. In a bout of anger from the floor of the state House, the fellow legislator challenged those opposing her to a metaphorical schoolyard brawl and said she'd meet them at 3:15 p.m. "after school."[4] It was a silly remark at the time, Pullen thought. But it's clear now why she was awoken in the middle of the night. Penny Pullen, a Republican, had become one of the principal opponents of ratification in Illinois, and her vocal opposition was garnering increased attention from ERA supporters and the media. She may have heard only silence on the other end of the phone, but the intended message was loud and clear. But despite the Molotov cocktails, shattered windows, and dead frogs, Pullen remained unyielding in her opposition to the proposal.

Pullen represented a suburban community nestled between O'Hare International Airport and the northwest side of Chicago. Mostly white, the district varied economically from middle-class to wealthy suburbanites. It was the kind of place where residents took the commuter train to the bustling city for work each morning and came home to a quiet 1950s bungalow or ranch home constructed in the postwar boom. Viewed from the vantage point of the planes flying in and out of nearby O'Hare Airport, Pullen's district was filled with cookie-cutter neighborhoods divided down the middle by miles of forest preserve running along the Des Plaines River. It was a picturesque area by most suburban standards.

Since being introduced in Congress, the Equal Rights Amendment had faced a rocky road. The amendment was passed on March 22, 1972, by the U.S. Senate and sent to the states for full ratification. First conceived by suffragist Alice Paul, the proposal was studied for decades before it garnered a serious chance at passage.[5] It faced opposition initially from organized labor and middle-class women who feared it would eliminate some of the privileges they enjoyed under various laws such as those regulating hours and working conditions for women or a court's inclination to favor women in child custody battles and claims for alimony. Pullen echoed this view. "I think women are discriminated against and discriminated for. I think it balances out," she later noted during a TV interview.[6]

Article V of the Constitution requires ratification of three-fourths of the state legislatures for an amendment to be approved. Mostly uncontentious at the time, the ERA passed overwhelmingly in Congress with bipartisan support. Some states even began the work of ratification that very day. Hawaii, with six hours separating it between Washington, took just a few hours to rubber stamp the amendment in both of its legislative chambers. President Richard Nixon lauded the amendment after it passed through Congress and urged fellow Republicans to support it as well. Indeed, the ERA was one of the few uncontroversial things in Washington for most of its existence.

But after leaving Washington, it didn't matter what Congress or the president thought of the ERA. The fate of the amendment would now be determined by legislators in a handful of state capitals across the country. While many states were quick to move, the ratification process stalled after a few years and by 1980, proponents were just three states short of the three-fourths required. Illinois quickly became the bloodiest battleground.

The Illinois General Assembly first took up the measure in 1972 and swiftly rejected it. And then again in 1973. And 1974. And every subsequent year leading up to 1980. Some years the state House passed it. Other years the state Senate passed it. But year after year, supporters of the ERA had failed thus far to muster enough backing in both legislative chambers necessary for passage.

Adding to this difficulty, Illinois was home to the ERA's most prominent foe: Phyllis Schlafly. Supporters of the ERA contended that Phyllis Schlafly was a woman of contradictions. Perhaps more accurately, they thought she was a power-hungry hypocrite. A mother of six, Schlafly was a highly educated woman with a master's degree. She ran for Congress twice as a Republican in Illinois but was unsuccessful. Schlafly later traveled the country speaking as a political activist focused mostly on national security issues like nuclear arms control. A prodigious writer, she penned the book *A Choice Not an Echo*, which many political observers credited with helping conservative icon and Arizona senator Barry Goldwater win the Republican presidential nomination in 1964.[7] Unsatisfied with her master's degree, she went back to school and at the age of fifty-three earned her law degree from Washington University in St. Louis.

During one of her campaign events while running for Congress in 1970, Schlafly told a room of supporters, "My opponent says a woman's place is in the home. But my husband replies that a woman's place is in the House—the United States House of Representatives."[8] And yet, despite the cheeky one-liner and her ambitious career, Schlafly became symbolic of the homemakers who feared what ERA would do to their way of life. She formed the main opposition group to the amendment—STOP ERA—when she convened a group of women at the O'Hare Airport Inn in 1972 to strategize.[9] The name stood for "Stop Taking Our Privileges," which illustrated the group's argument that the Equal Rights Amendment would send women into combat, create single-sex bathrooms, and take away alimony payments in a divorce. They feared it would have implications for abortion laws and open the door to gay rights too. The group had power, and Phyllis Schlafly had a mailing list of thousands of women across the country who shared her concerns. "I really think I have more power right here—with this organization—than I would as a senator," she once told a group of women gathered for a STOP ERA training event.[10] Even to her greatest detractor, this was true. The bigger her opposition grew, the more powerful she became.

Behind Phyllis Schlafly, Penny Pullen was one of the most prominent women standing up against the ERA in Illinois. And like Schlafly, she too was a woman of contradictions in the eyes of her detractors. A self-proclaimed profamily advocate, Pullen was single and had no children. She was one of twin girls in the Pullen family. And while her sister Pam left Park Ridge and started a family, Pullen stayed at home. By now a grown woman in her thirties, she continued living with her parents in the home she was raised in since moving to Park Ridge in 1960. A profile in the *Chicago Sun-Times* would describe her years later as a "spinster," a term that today would cause an uproar if used by a mainstream publication. And although Pullen was concerned principally with protecting the family unit, she also recognized being single allowed her to devote more time and energy toward her career.

Elected in 1976 at the age of twenty-nine, she replaced her former boss, State Representative Robert Juckett, who passed away from cancer while she was working for him as a legislative aide in Springfield. She was unsatisfied with the candidates vying to replace him—viewing them as insufficiently conservative—and decided to run herself. She contacted local party officials, knocked on doors, and eventually garnered the support of local party officials in her heavily Republican district. To stand out among the field of candidates, Penny Pullen sent out campaign mailers to voters in the district with a single penny glued to the front. It was a creative way to increase her name recognition and a sure-fire method for encouraging voters to read the piece instead of tossing it in the trash.

Pullen's experience in electoral politics first began when she volunteered for Juckett's opponent in the Republican primary as a teenager. When her candidate lost, she jumped on board with Juckett and eventually became an aide in his district office in Park Ridge. In time, she became close enough with Juckett to travel with him back and forth to Springfield. During legislative session, she would even help write bills after learning the process and becoming familiar with the legalese that comes along with drafting legislation.

In 1965, Pullen had headed to the University of Illinois at Chicago Circle to study journalism. The campus on which she studied had been a vibrant Italian neighborhood before being torn down by Mayor Richard J. Daley to build a campus to accommodate baby boomers seeking an education. Quickly, Pullen gave up her early flirtations with becoming a reporter and took an interest in politics.

Pullen was unflinchingly self-assured. She spoke with a stern tone and seemed never in doubt about the principles for which she stood. Standing at average height, she had short, deep red hair, which she wore in a bob or sometimes curly. She used little makeup but had a naturally youthful face. She was serious. Critics would portray her as harsh, almost perpetually irritated at anyone who would question the validity of what she said; supporters adored her sense of clear direction. When she spoke, Pullen enunciated her words clearly. She took brief pauses to think and ensure that each word coming out of her mouth had its intended purpose and meaning—never an "um" to fill space. Descriptions of her politics ran the gamut, from "intense" to "fanatical."[11] To many of her more supportive colleagues, she was just practical and understood the meaning of political power. Penny Pullen was the kind of politician you either loved or hated.

STOP ERA and Phyllis Schlafly aimed to tug on the heartstrings of legislators by leaning on emotional arguments about women heading into combat or men using women's bathrooms. The group was best known for baking cookies and bread adorned with creative slogans like "Preserve us from a congressional jam; vote against the ERA sham!"[12] At rallies and while lobbying members in the Illinois General Assembly, the group would pass out sweets as a reminder of where the homemakers in their district stood on the ERA.

Pullen, on the other hand, was a technocrat. She was most concerned with the more obscure Section 2 enforcement clause of the amendment that stated: "The Congress shall have the power to enforce, by appropriate legislation, the provisions of this article."[13] She was worried that this language, found in places in the Constitution such as the Fourteenth Amendment, would create a new enumerated power leading to massive overreach from the federal government. Pullen had spent her career as a legislative aide and at the levels of government closest to the citizens; she was concerned the clause would take power from the local elected officials who best understood the needs of their constituents.

Despite slight differences on what they viewed as the central problem of the ERA, Pullen and Schlafly both agreed the amendment would be a disaster for the country. The two had become close acquaintances, speaking on the phone occasionally or discussing the issues of the day over a meal. "She's good at politics; she likes politics. That makes her fun for me," Schlafly said of her friend Pullen. "We go out to dinner and discuss politics all night long. She's open to new ideas, but she has principles and she sticks by them."[14]

Pullen tried to remain involved in the STOP ERA movement whenever she could. At a conference in October of 1979, Pullen spoke to a crowd of 300 women gathered in St. Louis across the river from where Schlafly lived. She reassured the women of the impact they were having and the importance of continuing to fight against the ERA. "You are committed to the right things," she told them. "You will keep America moving toward the light."[15] Pullen, like the women she sought to motivate, was a dedicated soldier for the cause.

The STOP ERA movement was thoroughly organized. At events like the one in St. Louis, thousands of women were educated on the issues the organization believed were central concerns to the country, from abortion to gay rights to national defense. Activists gathered to dine and learned how to engage politically. They learned how to fundraise and host brunches to raise money, how to write letters to their local newspapers and reach out to their elected officials. They even learned how to testify at public hearings but were cautioned "never say you represent an organization" so the movement could appear grassroots in nature.[16] Detractors may have mocked these women as mere housewives, but their group was quickly becoming difficult to counter.

Pullen first met Schlafly at a rally in the capitol rotunda in Springfield where every year the ERA was introduced, they had helped to defeat it on their home turf. While Schlafly and her supporters baked bread and cookies, Pullen kept her head down and focused on legislating. She was more likely to be found on the House floor than at home making treats in the kitchen.

Rallies became a common feature around the state capital since the first year the ERA failed to advance in Springfield. On one occasion, televangelist Jerry Falwell came to town to host one on the steps of the capitol. Falwell had become a very public figure among conservative Christians through his *Old-Time Gospel Hour* program broadcast directly from his Baptist church in Lynchburg, Virginia, to living rooms across the nation. He further cemented his status as political force on the right after forming the Moral Majority, a group that encouraged Christians to make their voices heard in the political arena. Armed with his newfound celebrity, Falwell was traveling to all fifty states and hosting "I Love America" rallies in state capitals. His message was simple: America is in moral decline and our nation needs an awakening.

Falwell's involvement marked an about-face of sorts because he believed adamantly for years that preachers had no business involving themselves in the affairs of the state. The pulpit was a sacred place, he thought, and it was not to be defiled by getting down and dirty with the donkeys and the elephants. His view quickly transformed in 1973 after the Supreme Court legalized abortion nationwide in *Roe v. Wade*.[17] Falwell, like many Americans, believed it was a sign of the country's moral descent, and he placed the ERA in the same basket of issues threatening to drag the nation down.

The "I Love America" rallies had the ostentatious flair of a tent revival. Thousands gathered at events that blurred the lines between religion and politics. They sang songs and heard from political luminaries about the pressing issues. Signs at the events dotted the crowd with messages like "No Foxholes for My Daughter" and "Don't Draft Our Daughters."[18]

In the weeks leading up to the Springfield rally, advertisements from Falwell's Moral Majority appeared in newspapers across the state. Three central figures adorned the ads: Falwell, Schlafly, and Penny Pullen. Falwell, the preacher, cautioned of the ERA as "an attack upon the family and the Bible." Schlafly, the activist, warned of "a vote to draft young women and assign them to military combat equally with men." And Pullen, the wonky legislator, stuck to her talking points about impending federal government overreach.[19]

• • •

On May 14, 1980, pro-ERA demonstrators gathered in the capitol rotunda to show their support for ratification. Above the crowd were the stained-glass windows of the dome's summit, through which light shined like a colorful kaleidoscope. Surrounding the crowd were the ornate, beige-toned murals recounting the story of the state's past. In the middle of it all where each floor met around the center of the building to create a well, a bronze sculpture called *Illinois Welcoming the World* depicted a woman holding her arms wide open to all passing by. Both sides of the debate had become regular fixtures in this stately capitol setting, so this gathering was certainly nothing out of the ordinary. Pullen passed the demonstrators to and from meetings and hearings throughout the day. The legislative session was set to end in a few weeks and those gathered were eager for a vote on the issue.

Seeing the original seven-year deadline approach, Congress had extended it from March 22, 1979, to June 30, 1982, to provide state legislatures extra time. To many, the date of the extension seemed odd: June 30, 1982. Given the previous deadline was March 22, 1979, the most straightforward change would have been to extend the date by a simple three years. Why June? What was so special about those extra 100 days? To anyone paying close attention, the answer was clear. The Illinois General Assembly's legislative session was slated to finish at the end of June, and national supporters of the ERA had their eyes on the Land of Lincoln.

One of Pullen's fellow legislators, State Representative Nord Swanstrom, passed through the crowd throughout the day as well. At one point, he stopped to speak to a group of pro-ERA demonstrators who were gathered under the rotunda. He heard the women out but made it clear that he was leaning toward opposing the measure. Swanstrom was a freshman legislator mere months into the job who represented a mostly rural district three hours west of Chicago. Barely thirty, his hair was cleanly cut and carefully parted on the side, which helped to mask the baby-faced look he had when compared to some of his more experienced colleagues.

As he walked away from the group of pro-ERA activists, a woman approached him and slipped a business card into his suit pocket. Representative Swanstrom pulled out the card and flipped it to the back. "Mr. Swanstrom—The offer for help in your election and $1,000 for your campaign for pro-ERA vote," it read.[20] The rookie legislator was stunned. Unsure of what to do, he took the card to his boss, the house minority leader, who proceeded to report it to the police.

Wanda Brandstetter was a longtime volunteer for the National Organization for Women who had come down from Chicago to show her support for the ERA. The fifty-five-year-old mother of three was a biologist by profession and ardent feminist. She was dedicated to her cause, but she had just made a fatal mistake.

When Brandstetter returned to her home in Chicago, she was greeted by investigators who questioned her. She was eventually indicted for bribery and faced a hefty fine and community service. To ERA supporters, she was a martyr for the cause who was guilty of nothing more than being an amateur. Phyllis Schlafly's STOP ERA had, after all, donated tens of thousands of dollars to the campaigns of various state legislators with clear intentions. But no matter how the insiders looked at it, it was another strike against the pro-ERA movement. Being less organized than the other side was not an excuse. Pullen found the incident to be yet another display of the foul tactics the pro-ERA supporters used to promote their cause, a view that was shared by an increasing number of Illinoisans.

Aside from the attempted bribery, which caused a delay in the proceedings, public support in Illinois was beginning to wane. A *Chicago Tribune* poll in May of 1980 showed that 40 percent of voters favored the amendment while 37 percent opposed.[21] For a long time, the proposal was overwhelmingly popular with the public, but it seemed the tactics of supporters were beginning to take a toll on the public view of the issue.

For Pullen, however, the polls were not all great news. The *Tribune* survey found that support for ERA was highest in suburbs like the district she represented. Some local constituents took note of her vocal opposition. "Perhaps this stems in part from our misfortune in having male chauvinistic females like Phyllis Schlafly and Penny Pullen as political activists from this state," wrote one constituent opining on the ERA's legislative troubles.[22] But Pullen didn't let a few bad poll numbers or angry letters dictate where she'd come down on such an important issue.

On June 18, 1980, the time had come for a final vote of the session on ERA. All the efforts of demonstrators, local leaders, and even President Jimmy Carter were coming to the forefront. Supporters of the ERA arrived at the capitol at 10 a.m. dressed in green and white while opponents wore red to symbolize their disagreement. Pullen found the antics somewhat comical. There was national press attention and constant hoopla throughout the capitol, but no one ever lobbied her. They knew exactly where she stood.

From the Oval Office, President Carter worked the phones calling undecided legislators in the morning urging them to support ratification.[23] For these lawmakers who were technically serving in a part-time position, receiving a call from the leader of the free world was a big deal. From city hall in Chicago, Mayor Jane Byrne called legislators to whip up last-minute support as well. She had become a regular presence in the weeks leading up to the vote. As the mayor of America's second largest city and one of the most powerful women in the country, her voice carried weight on this issue.

While the capitol spun into chaos and aides rushed furiously throughout the hallways, legislative pages brought in hot dogs for the legislators to feast on while they awaited the vote. When the time came, Pullen entered the House floor and hit the red button on her desk indicating her decision. At 6:45 p.m., the lights on the voting board of the House floor were all lit up—102 green and 71 red.[24] The amendment failed, just five votes short of the three-fifths total required by the General Assembly's rules. For the seventh time, Illinois had rejected the Equal Rights Amendment.

• • •

After a crushing defeat in 1980, ERA supporters knew that 1982 would be their last chance at success. When the clock struck midnight on June 30, the extended deadline granted by Congress would expire and the proposed Twenty-seventh Amendment would be dealt its final blow.

Supporters developed a strategy to break the logjam in a number of states. By 1982, the National Organization for Women (NOW) was better organized and financed than during previous defeats. They had wised up to the tactics of ERA opponents and were ready for a final showdown. With 450,000 donors across the country, the group prepared to launch a multimillion-dollar television and newspaper advertising campaign in support of their case. They put forth a direct mail effort in Illinois and planned to lobby legislators heavily. Rallies were planned for Florida, Oklahoma, and North Carolina, some of the few remaining outliers. The ERA needed just three more states to pass. Above all, Illinois remained the main prize.

NOW and the legislators driving the issue wanted to remain focused on the substance of the amendment. It meant equality for women under the law, not all the crazy attacks critics were leveling against the amendment. But as the process began, keeping the focus on substance proved difficult. Seven women from out of state entered the capitol in late May of 1982 and declared they were going on a hunger strike. Drinking only water, they held a vigil and vowed to not eat until the ERA was ratified or the June 30 deadline passed.

The women came from disparate religious backgrounds. Sonia Johnson was a Mormon who was allegedly excommunicated from the church for her support of the Equal Rights Amendment. Within a few weeks, she became too weak to stand and was confined to a wheelchair in the capitol. Later, Johnson was brought to a nearby hospital in Springfield by one of her fellow activists who collapsed upon arrival. They had both lasted twenty-one days.[25]

Another demonstrator, a nun, compared her hunger strike experience to "like being an animal in the zoo, but no one throws any peanuts."[26] They sat on the hard marble floor of the capitol and occasionally broke out into song. One woman started going blind. "It's like looking through a kaleidoscope," she told a reporter. "Everything is moving, but I can't stop the motion."[27]

The hunger strike frustrated ERA supporters. One pro-ERA legislator vowed to withhold his vote until the women ceased their fast. These seven women were willing to risk their health for the fate of women's equality, but they had no connection to the state, were not in coordination with the larger campaign, and had turned the legislative process into a circus.

Shortly after the hunger strike began, fourteen women then decided to chain themselves to the doors of the state Senate chambers. The women stood in a group with shackles confining them to the area and called themselves the "Grassroots Group of Second Class Citizens." The group periodically broke out into song as cameras approached and chanted pro-ERA slogans for all to hear.

For the next few weeks, Pullen took additional precautions while at work to avoid getting caught up with the shenanigans. When entering the state House floor to take votes, she had a staffer sit in her chair on the floor and take directions. From a few rows back, out of the view of anyone watching from above in the gallery, she would signal her intention on each bill. Thumbs up for yes, thumbs down for no. As the General Assembly drew closer to voting on the ERA, Pullen wasn't taking any chances.

The final vote took place on June 25, 1982. In a bipartisan rejection, the amendment failed to advance from the Senate Executive Committee. At long last, the ERA went out not with a bang but with a whimper. After ratification in thirty-five states and passage in Congress, the measure failed to advance through a simple committee vote in Springfield.

Immediately following the vote, chaos erupted in the capitol. Nine women from the Grassroots Group of Second Class Citizens rushed over to the governor's office and spilled pig's blood they had obtained from a local butcher all over the white marble floors. With red blood they spelled the names out of legislators who had let them down.[28]

Pro-ERA demonstrators gathered under the capitol rotunda, locked arms, and began singing "We Shall Overcome" in unison. Pullen would have none of it. Surrounded by supporters, she began to sing a patriotic song of her own and belted the opening lyrics of "God Bless America."[29] She wasn't about to let them have even a symbolic victory. Likeminded demonstrators joined in and attempted to drown out the political adversaries they had fought long and hard to defeat.

Schlafly, Pullen, and all those opposing ratification in Illinois had indeed won. The proposed Twenty-seventh Amendment to the United States Constitution was dead. Penny Pullen, however, was just getting started.

Rosemary Mulligan in 1990. Photo Credit: Matthew Bonaguidi

2

Rosemary Mulligan

Things happen in life that aren't planned or pleasant,
but we learn to be survivors.

On July 8, 1941, the lead story of the *Chicago Daily Tribune* announced the U.S. Navy's occupation of Iceland in an effort to prevent a Nazi takeover of the territory. Just below, the paper declared that the "British Believe Americans Will Guard Atlantic" despite many Americans' lingering reticence to enter the conflict raging across the ocean. Amid the forest of text, a political cartoon depicted five greedy men gathered around a table in black tailcoat suits representing European nations' "shameful ingratitude" for America's previous effort in World War I. While the editorial board of the *Tribune* might have felt confident in the country's ability to stay on the sidelines, the nation would soon be dragged into the war just a few months later following the Japanese attack on Pearl Harbor.

On this day, Rose and Stephen Granzyk welcomed their daughter Rosemary into the chaotic world depicted on the front page of the *Tribune*. The Granzyk family spent their early child-rearing years living in various Chicago neighborhoods, eventually ending up long term in the community of Albany Park on the city's north side. The couple rented a cramped attic apartment above Rose's parents during a period in which the country's then-second largest city was experiencing rapid growth. In 1941, the skyscrapers that today adorn the city skyline could only be imagined in a work of fiction. Pedestrians traversed the city using its extensive network of electric streetcars that would in time be replaced by the more modern Chicago "L" trains. Just south of the city's downtown area, the Union Stock Yards were still a humming district of meatpackers that formed the core of the country's food-processing industry. And the city's mayor, Edward J. Kelly, oversaw a political fiefdom beholden to the rough-and-tumble machine politics for which the area would later become infamous.

Rosemary was the couple's first child, and she would be joined by her younger brother Stephen just four years later. During her adolescence, Rosemary joyfully took on the role of a supportive big sister. She was friendly, playing sports in the neighborhood with the boys and the girls alike. To some, Rosemary was a bit of a tomboy. She had a hearty sense of humor and was easygoing, the kind of kid who could easily fit in with whatever group was around. From an early age, Rosemary became known for her honesty and bluntness, a brashness that could sometimes turn into a temper. Rosemary didn't wear her heart on her sleeve, but she also never shied away from letting others know exactly how she felt.

After years of city life, the Granzyks eventually decided to take their young family to the suburbs in search of more room and a space separate from Rose's parents. With careful planning, the couple managed to scrape up enough money in 1950 for a down payment on their first home in the far western suburb of Glen Ellyn. Completed without plumbing or electricity, their new home was slowly fixed up by Rosemary's father while her mother filled the space with secondhand furniture and other used items given by family.[1]

In 1955 at age fourteen, Rosemary and her family moved to nearby suburban Park Ridge, an up-and-coming suburb on the northwest border of the city. Like many families in postwar Chicago, the Granzyks moved in search of a home and the promise of good public schools. "It is one of the oldest towns in Cook County," a real estate advertisement from the time said of Park Ridge. "Departing from the usual square cut plan, the little city is laid out in miles of circling drives overhung with great elms and maples making it a veritable fairy land."[2] As with most suburbs at the time, Park Ridge was almost entirely white and quickly growing, with the city building its first fire station in 1955 when the Granzyks moved there.

At the time, a plot of land in the area was still far larger than one would find in a modern suburb, with unpaved roads and small amounts of crops or chickens clucking about in a homeowner's yard not an unusual sight. The Granzyks settled for a smaller abode, purchasing a newly constructed two-story brick townhouse with three bedrooms on the south end of the city on Higgins Road. It was a modest setting compared to the much larger single-family bungalows or Victorian-style homes nearby, but it provided a much-awaited sense of stability for the Granzyks. They shared walls with other neighbors at the neatly organized complex with a communal yard and a garage jutting up against an alley. Quiet and calm when the Granzyks first moved there, the area would become increasingly busy with the opening of O'Hare Airport to commercial travel and the construction of the Northwest Expressway just yards away (eventually renamed the Kennedy Expressway).

Rosemary's father, Stephen Granzyk, worked much of his life as a carpenter and cabinetmaker with skills that he'd fine-tuned during time spent as part of the Civilian Conservation Corps, a New Deal—era program aimed at lowering unemployment for young men. Born in Chicago, he was a handsome man who stood at five feet, six inches. Stephen's parents had emigrated from Poland and often struggled to make ends meet raising their eleven children during the Great Depression. Over the years, Stephen remained an active part of his local labor union, a passionate advocate at the grassroots level for the rights of workers. Eventually Stephen would have a short-lived crack at the insurance business and was hired by American National Insurance Company for a stint as a salesman, a job that gave the family the opportunity for a middle-class living.

Rosemary's mother Rose also worked in addition to caring for the children, handling accounts payable at a local refrigeration business called RMC Inc. The family would later open a greeting card store on the northwest side of Chicago, which she and her husband ran. Born in Chicago to Italian parents, Rose was just four foot eleven but full of personality. Rose had contracted polio at eighteen months old, which left one of her arms mostly unusable.[3] But she was an iron-willed woman also shaped by her family's struggles during the Depression, and she never let her disability weigh her down. "If I can do this with one good arm, you can do it with two," she'd tell her children.[4] Rose used it as an opportunity to imbue in her family a sense of empathy for those from different backgrounds.

Now a teenager, Rosemary began attending Maine Township High School about five miles northwest of their new home for her sophomore year in 1957. Because of the rapid growth of the surrounding area, the halls of the school were packed with more than 4,500 students as families continued flocking to the suburbs. By the end of Rosemary's time as a student there, the school would be renamed Maine East after other facilities were constructed in the district to meet the demand following World War II.[5]

Maine Township was a typical high school of the late 1950s. Boys wore button-down long-sleeve shirts and pressed slacks. Girls donned simple collared blouses and circle skirts, often cut from felt with a design added for some flair—a modest floral pattern or polka dots as an accent. Male teachers were almost always found in a full suit and tie, a further testament to the formality of dress during the era.

The decade marked an increase in educational and vocational opportunities for women, with many heading to college after graduation. Still, it was not uncommon to walk the halls and see an entirely female class clacking away on typewriters or mastering their shorthand during a stenography course all in anticipation for a position in the secretarial pool. The role of the school was to prepare women for the jobs that were available, not necessarily those to which they might aspire.

Homecoming at Maine Township was a much-anticipated affair, with student clubs decorating floats for a kick-off parade, a queen crowned by her admiring peers, and boys with slicked-back hair dressed in letter jackets with an oversized "M" on the front. All in all, the average student looked fit for a role as an extra in the movie *Grease*.

Despite having moved to a new town and changing schools for her sophomore year, Rosemary made fast friends. She did well in her studies, played field hockey, and participated in her grade's student council. To earn extra money on the side, Rosemary worked at a local dress shop in downtown Des Plaines. And when her free time allowed it, Rosemary would date here and there.

In time, Rosemary became acquainted with a boy in the grade above her. A football player, six feet tall with a flat-top haircut, Dan Bonaguidi and Rosemary quickly became high school sweethearts.[6] Bonaguidi graduated in 1958 and headed north to the University of Wisconsin in Madison.[7] Despite the two-hour distance between them, they remained a couple and continued dating seriously.

During her senior year, the time came for Rosemary to begin exploring her future. She decided her path was to become a teacher, one of the most common professions for women at the time. With the help of a high school guidance counselor, she obtained a scholarship and in 1959 headed south to Illinois State University in Normal, the state's oldest public university.[8] The city of Normal received its name because the institution was founded as a normal school, an establishment dedicated to training teachers. Rosemary decided to focus her studies on social science education.

But just a few years into his studies in Wisconsin, Dan Bonaguidi decided to join his father's insurance business, which he had founded in 1949 after coming home from war.[9] When Dan moved back to Illinois to join the family trade, Rosemary decided it was time to follow her high school sweetheart home. She had completed just a year of school, so her previous goal of becoming a teacher would be put on a permanent pause. For a few months, Rosemary joined her mother in a secretarial position at RMC Inc. Her focus would soon turn to the duty of wife and homemaker, with an eye toward building a family. The couple quickly got engaged in October of 1960 just weeks before the country narrowly chose Massachusetts Senator John F. Kennedy over Vice President Richard Nixon to lead the nation. Like the Kennedys, both Rosemary and Dan were Catholic. Nine months later in August of 1961, the two wed at a local Catholic church and Rosemary Granzyk became Rosemary Bonaguidi.[10]

Rosemary and Dan Bonaguidi settled down in the rapidly growing suburb of Des Plaines, just a few miles from where she had gone to high school. Like Park Ridge, the city of Des Plaines was experiencing a population boom, with construction replacing cornfields on a regular basis. New playgrounds for children, public pools to escape the summer heat, and restaurants, such as an up-and-coming drive-in burger joint called McDonald's opened by local businessman Ray Kroc, were all sprouting up surrounding the city's downtown area like spokes in a wheel.

The couple wasted little time building their life in Des Plaines, and within a month, Rosemary was pregnant with their first child. For both the Granzyks and the Bonaguidis, it was a joyous announcement because it would be the first grandchild for either side. Daniel "Danny" Bonaguidi was born in June of 1962 and quickly doted on by both sets of loving grandparents.[11]

Rosemary became a dedicated mother, throwing herself into the role of housewife with as much gusto as anything she'd done before. She cared for her new child and kept up the home, cooking, cleaning, and completing all the other tasks required of a busy homemaker. Rosemary was a loving parent with a playful and affectionate side for her child. But she also wasn't the type of parent who thought her child was infallible, and she never shied away from playing the role of disciplinarian.

Both Rosemary and Dan Bonaguidi's families lived close by, and the couple lived a normal life in the suburbs. But unfortunately for Rosemary, their idyllic world would soon face tragedy. In late November of 1967, Rosemary, Dan, and their five-year-old son were preparing for the holidays as in any year. But on the week of Thanksgiving, Rosemary's father agreed to pick up a shift during the short-staffed holiday week. He was tasked with picking up an insurance premium on the south side of Chicago in a housing project called Rockwell Gardens. Her father was mere weeks into his new job as a salesman.

Constructed just a decade earlier, the "Gardens" received its name from the flowers that early residents had planted to liven up the common areas surrounding the eight-building complex. Each apartment stood ten to thirteen stories tall and alternated red brick and gray concrete. Rockwell Gardens was part of a series of public housing projects that were spearheaded in the 1950s by Mayor Richard J. Daley. Originally praised as a revolutionary way to house low-income residents, Daley and other politicians used public housing as a way to further segregate the city and the projects were poorly maintained. Rosemary's father knew the area was dangerous, but he was also eager to leave a good impression in his newfound role and get the books in order for whoever would take on that route more permanently. What he didn't realize when he took the assignment at Rockwell Gardens was that his colleague usually came accompanied by an armed guard.[12]

Rosemary's father arrived alone at the designated apartment building and went to the fifth floor where he picked up the insurance premium from a woman. While he was collecting, five boys all aged seventeen and eighteen gathered in a nearby apartment. One of the boys took out a .22 caliber rifle with the barrel sawed off and displayed to the awe-struck group. He explained to the group that another friend had asked him to hold on to the weapon for a while. The boys passed it around, admiring its touch and feel until they were told to leave the apartment by one of the boy's sisters.

There was no talk of robbery when the boys were passing around the weapon, nor were they aware an insurance collector was inside the building. But when one of the boys saw Rosemary's father paused in the middle staircase of the complex, the idea to rob him clicked in their minds. "When I seen him I started looking at everybody else and everybody started looking at me," one of boys later recounted on the witness stand.[13] With the gun in hand, one of the boys followed Rosemary's father down the staircase while the others fanned out in nearby stairwells to trap him in place.

A shot rang out and he collapsed to the floor. Rosemary's father had been hit in the chest, and as he lay on the floor bleeding, the boys rifled through his pockets. In total, they took $35 and a wristwatch. All the perpetrators ran from the scene and one of the perpetrators hid the gun in his sister's dresser. The boys all divided the money, with $7 for each person. In perhaps a last-minute display of regret, one of the boys gave his share back to the group.

Rosemary's father had told his wife Rose to wait for him at the greeting card store after closing up for the night, promising to pick her up and drive home after he had finished his business at Rockwell Gardens. Rosemary's mother waited. And waited. But as the night dragged on, she began fearing for the worst. So, she called her daughter and son-in-law to pick her up and take her home for the night. The three of them waited anxiously back at the townhouse in Park Ridge until finally, a police squad car pulled up to their door and approached their stoop to deliver the news. At that moment, it became clear to everyone that something terrible had happened.

Thanksgiving was just a few days later, and what was normally a joyous occasion filled with family and fun was instead a day of mourning for Rosemary's family and preparation for a funeral the next day. "Why did he go in there?" Rosemary's mother would ask over and over seated at the kitchen table, rhetorically searching for answers to an unanswerable and mentally exhausting question.[14]

Eventually identified thanks to an anonymous tip, three of the boys—men by the time they faced trial—went to prison while the other two reached plea deals by agreeing to testify against their friends. The trials that took place in the years following the murder were long and exhausting for the family. Rosemary's mother, in particular, was devastated, and Rosemary attended as many of the proceedings as she could to accompany her through the gut-wrenching process, one of which eventually reached the Illinois Supreme Court. "It had a big impact on my life. Sitting through those trials and seeing what it did to my mom," she would later recount.[15]

When her mother's address was published in the paper by a reporter covering the murder trials, Rose Granzyk decided to move out of her home, the townhouse where Rosemary and her brother had grown up. The family feared for her safety and even more so, Rose preferred not to be alone following her husband's death. The whole ordeal put the smaller things into perspective for Rosemary. Later, when life's figurative trials reached a new low, she thought back to the literal trials that had haunted her family for so long.

By 1969, Rosemary was again pregnant with the couple's second child and in February of 1970, Matthew Bonaguidi was born. The year 1970 was characterized by increasing demonstrations in opposition to the war in Vietnam, the killing of four protestors at Kent State, and the much-watched trial of the Chicago Seven. For fans of the British rock sensation the Beatles, it also marked the end of their decade-long rise to fame as the band's relationship deteriorated. In roughly the same length of time, Rosemary and Dan also faced struggles in their relationship, and it eventually became clear their union wouldn't last. After eleven years, the couple split up while their children were aged two and twelve.[16]

Despite the divorce, they remained close friends and were cooperative parents raising the boys. While Rosemary may have been legally split from the family, she kept the Bonaguidis close. She remained in a neighborhood surrounded by her ex-husband's family so the boys could grow up around them. They lovingly referred to the area as "Bonaguidiville." Her ex's in-laws shared a backyard gate with her, her former sister-in-law lived next door, and her former brother-in-law was just three houses down as well.

Within a few years, Rosemary would enter her second marriage and take her new husband George's name—Mulligan. The two met through a single parent's group, with George's children now grown and fully out of the house by the time they wed. Of Irish descent with a lively sense of humor, George was a good-looking man of average height with a black head of hair just beginning the process of graying on both sides.

Despite the new nuptials, Rosemary and Dan Bonaguidi continued as amicable coparents and ensured the boys were surrounded by family at every turn. The two parents tried to stay involved in the community, with the boys playing Little League baseball, remaining active in the local Boy Scouts troop, and Rosemary volunteering her time to other causes where she could in addition to her duties as a wife and mother.

The Bonaguidis were a family of outdoorsmen. So, in September of 1982, Dan, his brother, and two other men decided to organize a moose hunting trip to Canada and hired a pilot to fly them to their destination.

Emil Mesich was an immigrant from southeast Europe who loved to fly, often helping tourists navigate the vast Canadian wilderness. But Mesich's record as a pilot was not without incident. Three years earlier in November of 1979, Mesich was set to carry a group of men back to Smithers, British Columbia, at the end of their vacation hunting trip.[17] Environmentally conscious, the men decided to take their leftover beer bottles on the plane. When loading them up, Mesich calculated that each case of empty bottles weighed about four pounds. But he had missed the mark by about three pounds, a seemingly minor miscalculation that meant the plane was actually more than 600 pounds over its weight limit.[18]

Mesich, along with his three passengers, got into the plane and prepared for liftoff. As the plane lifted off en route to their destination, the nose of the aircraft lifted toward the sky at an increasingly high angle. Suddenly, the engine began to stall. As he struggled to regain control of the aircraft, Emil and his passengers crashed to the ground. The force of the impact created a hungry fire that was quickly fed by the aircraft's fuel tank. By sheer luck, Mesich avoided the fire and was launched from the cockpit to an area clear of the flames. He survived, but his three passengers were quickly burned alive.[19]

This life-and-death experience might have forced some nonpilots to rethink the dangerous profession, but Mesich pressed on and in 1982 he was tasked with taking Dan Bonaguidi and the rest of his hunting party to Tatlatui Lake, a provincial park in British Columbia with popular fishing and hunting spots roughly equidistant from Anchorage and Seattle. His small, single-engine propeller plane was yellow with two brown stripes across the back wing.[20]

Mesich mapped out the canyon he would fly through so he could get the men to their destination. But as he got closer to the area he was supposed to fly over, Mesich realized the aircraft wasn't at a sufficient altitude. Knowing he had to act fast to avoid crashing, he pitched the aircraft in another direction. Two 200-liter drums of fuel aboard the aircraft weighed the plane down and it began scraping the tops of trees as it sunk back into the forest, breaking large branches on its descent before crashing into the ground. The aircraft ended up in a small clearing and folded like a crushed aluminum can upon impact as the wings ripped off. When the engine cooled and the propellers were finally motionless, the sounds of the forest returned to their natural tranquility. Unlike Mesich's previous crash, there was no fire. There were no flames. The massive fuel jugs that weighed them down didn't feed a raging inferno. But there were also no survivors. Just ten minutes after takeoff, Emil Mesich and his four passengers had died.[21]

When word reached the families of the men back in Illinois, the news was devastating. Calamity had again struck Rosemary's life, and it now meant she was the sole parent of her twelve- and twenty-year-old sons.

Around 1980, just a few years before the crash in Canada, Rosemary had made the decision to go back to school. When she and Dan decided to start a family years earlier, Rosemary had put her education on the back burner and never finished her schooling at Illinois State University. Rosemary decided to pursue an associate degree at Harper College, a local community college twenty minutes west of Des Plaines where she lived. She settled on a program in legal studies, a path that would allow her to find work as a paralegal. Juggling family life and obtaining a degree provided a unique challenge, so Rosemary would often bring her ten-year-old son Matt to the local library and busy him with homework or other activities while she was studying or conducting research. Her endeavor to obtain a degree was partly driven by an interest in finding something new and partly out of necessity. Rosemary could sense her second marriage with George Mulligan coming to an end, and she knew it was imperative that she lay the groundwork to find a decent job, pay her bills, and support her two boys.[22]

Around the time of Dan's death, Rosemary found a job at a law firm in the nearby city of Glenview called Miller, Forest, and Downing. She would spend most of her time on municipal law work, an area of the law that in many ways can tie in with local government and politics. On some weeknights, that meant attending zoning board meetings and getting to know local elected officials in the area.

After eight years of marriage, Rosemary and George had planned to announce their divorce to the boys but decided to hold off after the death of their father Dan. Both of them figured it wasn't fair having the boys lose two father figures in just one year. After another eighteen months, the two split and Mulligan officially became a single mother.

Naturally the death of Dan shook the entire family, but twenty-year-old Danny took his father's passing particularly hard. Losing a parent can be excruciating at any age, but it can be particularly difficult when occasioned by tragedy. Danny grew up an avid sports fan, someone who could rattle off the latest stats from the paper that morning and followed everything from football to tennis. He was known by some as a big personality with a big heart, the kind of guy who'd joke around during tennis practice in high school just to get a rise out of his teammates.[23] But as Danny got older, he began to develop problems with compulsive gambling that eventually led to trouble with the law.

It can be easy to assume that the worst addictions in life are those that affect you in more physical ways—drugs, alcohol, pills. But gambling, seemingly less nefarious, can easily become one of the most pervasive, destructive, and difficult addictions to overcome. When you're winning big and the numbers look good, gamblers get a high just like any other addict. When the going gets tough, however, the downward spiral can impact not just the person who's spending their own money with reckless abandon, but the family and friends around them. Aiding someone with addiction is like pulling a person out of quicksand. It's a task that's long, arduous, and sometimes futile. But a big-hearted person can't help but try.

Rosemary, like any supportive parent, was often the one pulled in to help clean up the mess her son had created. To the disinterested observer, the simple answer is often to let a person deal with his own demons and not get dragged into his trouble. But the answer is not that straightforward for those who love the addict.

Whether through tragic events or family dilemmas, Rosemary Mulligan's resilience had been constantly tested. "Things happen in life that aren't planned or pleasant, but we learn to be survivors," she later observed.[24]

· · ·

President Ronald Reagan shakes hands with Penny Pullen in Bethesda, Maryland, before announcing her as one of thirteen picks for the AIDS commission at the National Institutes of Health on July 23, 1987.
Photo Credit: Courtesy of the Ronald Reagan Presidential Library & Museum

3

Blood Terrorists

No man is an Iland, intire of itselfe . . .
any man's death diminishes me,
because I am involved in Mankinde.

Ronald Reagan had a problem. On June 24, 1987, the president signed Executive Order 12601 creating the Commission on the Human Immunodeficiency Virus Epidemic. The country had first become aware of the deadly AIDS virus in the summer of 1981, but the conversation surrounding the issue remained relatively muted as it spread across the country infecting Americans. Rumors about transmission abounded and many Americans believed falsely that the virus was airborne or could infect someone through saliva and sweat. Because of this, the administration was under growing pressure to act. By the time his commission was formed, AIDS had already infected 47,000 Americans.[1]

President Reagan was not alone in his reticence in discussing the virus. Newspaper and television coverage of the outbreaks was sparse the first few years as outlets were leery of covering a subject seen as taboo to many. The virus impacted segments of the population that much of mainstream society would rather pretend didn't exist. At first dubbed the "gay plague," AIDS mainly affected gay men and intravenous drug users who shared needles.

After the president's signing of the executive order, the White House's first task was to put together a list of people to fill the thirteen-member panel with the mission of advising the administration on the "medical, legal, ethical, social, and economic impact" of AIDS.[2] Aside from medical experts, the president needed cover for delving into what was becoming a thorny political issue. He needed to make sure that conservative voices were represented among the thirteen members and the final report it was tasked with creating didn't get out of hand with its recommendations. In search of those voices, the White House scoured lists of donors, legislators, and activists. By 1987, Phyllis Schlafly was a household name and a hero in conservative circles for helping defeat the ERA. So Schlafly was consulted on the matter. Who did she think would be a good fit to help craft a plan addressing the nation's most pressing public health crisis? Schlafly recommended two candidates for the job, but only one was placed: her old friend Penny Pullen.[3]

By 1987, Pullen had moved on from her ERA days and garnered significant attention in Illinois pushing AIDS-related bills in the General Assembly. She wanted the state to test all prisoners when they entered an institution and again during their routine physicals. She advocated for Illinois hospitals to test all patients aged thirteen to fifty-five and mandatory testing of sex offenders. She focused on mandatory contact tracing for those infected, something public health officials vehemently warned against because they believed it would result in people not coming forward for treatment.

In a post-COVID-19 world, contact tracing would seem like a no-brainer step to most Americans for combatting an infectious disease, but the stigma of AIDS added a layer of difficulty. Pullen viewed this as just one of many straightforward, tried-and-true public health tactics she was advancing. She had no patience for treating the disease as different from any other. "The public health people should almost have blinders on in terms of the social implications," she said in an interview with a conservative magazine.[4] But AIDS, in the eyes of most doctors and public health professionals, was a new problem with unique challenges. Critics of Pullen viewed it as further evidence she was more interested in leading a witch hunt than a public health campaign.

Most of Pullen's bills, despite being vehemently opposed by the medical community at-large in Illinois, passed the legislature and were signed by Governor Jim Thompson. Pullen had become adept at attaining legislative success in Springfield. Her success at actually addressing the public health crisis, however, was dubious.[5]

After the ERA fight and the attention it had brought her, Pullen was no stranger to criticism from the public. But the ERA had many central figures fighting the battle, which took the attention off her specifically. On AIDS, though, she was out front leading the charge. Her efforts garnered her particular attention from Chicago's gay community, making her a target of activists locally. Despite the pushback, Pullen insisted she was on an earnest mission to save their lives.

"Is there any public health official anywhere who will cite the biblical warning to those still actively courting death through what these officials call merely an 'alternative lifestyle,' the prediction in Paul's letter to the Romans: 'Men committed indecent acts with other men, and received in themselves the due penalty for their perversion'?" she asked rhetorically in a letter to supporters. Much of Pullen's criticism was aimed at the state's public health director, Dr. Barney Turnock.

During a public health crisis, officials like Turnock take on a very public-facing role, and Pullen was his highest-profile critic. At one point, Pullen bestowed upon Dr. Turnock the "Tinkerbell Award," a fake accolade meant to ridicule his handling of the crisis. "Just as in Peter Pan, Director Turnock thinks that if he shuts his eyes and slaps his hands and wishes 'real hard,' everything will turn out okay," she wrote in a press release. "This isn't Never-Never Land."

Pullen and Turnock would continue to brawl throughout the crisis, both lobbying the governor behind each other's back to either sign or veto various pieces of AIDS legislation. During a speech before his fellow public health directors at the Association of State and Territorial Health Officials, Turnock explained how Pullen's public disparagement affected him. "Not since my fourth-grade teacher—Sister Claudia—have I run up against someone of such intensity and zeal and such a truly intimidating personality."[6]

Pullen's most controversial piece of legislation was a bill that required mandatory AIDS testing for any couple applying for a marriage license in Illinois. Within thirty days of applying, soon-to-be newlyweds had to draw blood and send the results off to the state. The program was a disaster. In the first year of implementation, the state discovered only 26 cases out of nearly 160,000 marriage applications.[7] And in the end, most of those discovered were IV drug users. Illinois was the only state in the union with an AIDS marriage testing law, a contrast that prompted one legislator to declare Illinois "the laughingstock of the nation."[8] Monogamy was a foolproof way to prevent the spread, so why spend millions testing married couples? But Pullen pressed on. She defeated three separate attempts to repeal the marriage testing measure. During the 1987 session a total of fifty-seven AIDS bills passed the Illinois General Assembly, many of them shepherded across the finish line by Pullen.[9]

As a result of the marriage law, license applications in the state dropped about 25 percent.[10] Couples found it easier to cross the border instead of submitting themselves to a state-mandated blood test. Ten miles across the state's northern border in Wisconsin, the Kenosha Twins, a minor league baseball team, hosted a mass wedding ceremony on field for fourteen couples that summer, thirteen of whom were from Illinois. Just a year later, that number would soar to over 700 statewide. One bride noted, "We thought it was a silly law, and we decided why bother with it?"[11] The law would eventually be repealed when, after twenty-one months in effect, it uncovered just 52 positives out of 250,000 people tested.[12] For Pullen, the failure of the program was due to an ineffective public health department, not bad lawmaking.

The state had little success in addressing the AIDS crisis with other tactics either. Illinois's public health director sought to raise awareness of safe sex practices, so in April of 1987 the state health department released a rap song about the importance of condom use called the "Condom Rag." The jingle and surrounding campaign cost the taxpayers more than $450,000 to produce.[13] It was first revealed to the public at a mall in downtown Springfield. A five-person ensemble from Chicago called Local Talent performed the ditty at the mall atrium in front of an audience. "You say you want sex that's safe and fun? / Well, jive with us and we'll show you how it's done. / . . . Pardon the pun it's in the bag, / all you gotta do is the condom rag." The song was a bust. "It's garbage, plain garbage," the governor told a group of reporters at a press conference when asked about it.[14] He was embarrassed. Some Illinoisans thought the song made light of a serious public health crisis. Others thought it was inappropriate to be discussing condom use in such public places.

Despite Illinois's floundering, the Reagan administration thought Penny Pullen could bring a legislative perspective to the AIDS panel. Reagan aides lauded her as an example of someone who'd seen success in addressing the issue, and her experience in the legislature would be invaluable for the AIDS panel.

To those just discovering her, Pullen was a nobody. But to those who knew her, she was a heavyweight among social conservatives with rock-solid credentials. For critics, every time Pullen got involved in a cause she only made matters worse. The prospect of her having a voice in such an important issue nationally was unfathomable to them.

When asked to serve on the commission, Pullen accepted the appointment and traveled to Washington, DC, for the announcement. "If we accomplish something, I can be proud of having served. But this is a challenge and a responsibility—an awesome responsibility, not fluff and flowers," she told a local reporter before heading east.[15] The panel gathered in Bethesda, Maryland, at the National Institutes of Health on July 23, 1987. The visit began with President Reagan touring the facilities and highlighting how the virus was impacting everyday Americans. The president met with four children who had AIDS and gave each of them a jar of Jelly Belly jellybeans adorned with his signature and the presidential seal. He held a fourteen-month-old girl in his arms who had contracted the virus from her mother who was an IV drug user. He shook the hands of a preschooler who was infected from a blood transfusion.

Reagan's message was clear: He wanted people to understand that transmission was not as simple as just shaking hands or being in contact with others. He had been slow to start, but he now meant business. Despite very little infection among children, he kept the focus on protecting youngsters and avoided mentioning the populations that the virus impacted most. Before the press event where each panelist would be introduced to the nation, President Reagan entered a green room where the thirteen commissioners were gathered. One by one, he shook their hands and thanked them for agreeing to take on the assignment. Pullen admired Reagan a great deal. When she attended his first inauguration and saw him speak to the nation on the West Front of the Capitol, she burst out in tears of joy. Still, Pullen did not think Reagan was infallible as some conservatives did. "I don't have many human heroes," she told a reporter upon the appointment. "When anyone is compared to Jesus Christ they fall short."[16]

When the president finished chatting with Pullen and the other commissioners, he entered the room that was put together for a press conference unveiling his appointments. On the U-shaped dais, Pullen sat along with members of the commission while the president spoke. Wearing a baby blue dress and with her hands folded, she listened intently as the president alluded to the death of "friends and former associates" from AIDS and said he wanted to send the disease "the way of smallpox and polio."[17]

When Reagan finished his remarks, he turned the mic over to Dr. Anthony Fauci, director of the National Institute of Allergy and Infectious Diseases. The forty-six-year-old immunologist had been at the helm of the institute for just under three years and was tasked with overseeing the NIH's research on infectious diseases. Fauci first came to NIH in 1968 and had worked his way up to leading one of the agency's most important institutes. In the early 1980s, he heard about a strange new virus that was impacting gay men in a small group of urban areas around the country. By 1985, he was heading up all research related to AIDS at NIH. He decided to dedicate most of his efforts to studying the virus, and many of his colleagues thought he was foolish for focusing on what some saw as a trivial problem. And he had taken his fair share of criticism on the issue from activists who believed he wasn't doing enough to help combat the disease.[18]

After climbing the steps on stage, Dr. Fauci made his way to an easel that outlined NIH's efforts so far in battling the virus. Gripping a microphone in his left hand and a long, black pointer in his right, he discussed ongoing vaccine research and the five categories he believed made the AIDS virus a unique challenge. "Once the function of the genes is known, you can then make manipulations to interfere with the function of the virus," he told the crowd.[19] It was complex stuff, and most of the newly appointed commissioners were ill-equipped to understand such a presentation.

There are hundreds of commissions in Washington that touch every issue from energy to education, and most of these presidential panels receive little to no attention. But the AIDS commission was different, and all eyes were on this panel. Nightly news coverage of the event focused specifically on Pullen's appointment. She was described as an acolyte of "anti-gay hardliner Phyllis Schlafly."[20] The front page of the *Washington Post* the next day noted unfounded comments Pullen made accusing gay men of purposefully contaminating blood banks with AIDS-infected donations. "Blood terrorism," Pullen called it.[21]

• • •

In Illinois, reaction to Pullen's appointment was harsh. "Those in the know believe the commission is another bunch of idiots appointed for political, doctrinaire reasons who will produce a report everybody will laugh at," remarked a Chicago physician known for his treatment of AIDS patients. "[Pullen]'s irrational and inconsistent. She's hypocritical about her desire to control the epidemic," he insisted. "No panel at all would be preferable to the one we've got," remarked another doctor involved in the AIDS effort.[22]

Despite the public opprobrium surrounding her and others' selection, the president's thirteen-member panel would be tasked with crafting a report with recommendations to address the nation's most pressing public health crisis. The panel was a hodgepodge of individuals with varying levels of medical experience, if any at all. There was little experience among the group in treating patients with AIDS, nor were there members with experience in the sphere of testing or research. But the Reagan administration insisted this was the goal all along, to form a panel of various viewpoints that represented a wide spectrum of American experiences rather than just a body of medical experts. The administration wanted a report that could be communicated to everyday Americans as well as provide broader public health recommendations.

One of the first panelists was Dr. Theresa Crenshaw, a sex therapist from San Diego and frequent talk show guest. Before being appointed one of just thirteen commissioners, Dr. Crenshaw pushed for San Diego's public schools to deny AIDS-infected children admission to class. Crenshaw was a regular on talk shows in California and on many occasions—despite medical evidence to the contrary—informed viewers that AIDS could be transmitted through mosquitoes, pets, workers handling food, and even by using public toilets.[23] The phones lit up whenever Dr. Crenshaw was a guest on local TV warning the public they were all at risk. One talk show guest who appeared with Crenshaw, a doctor at San Francisco General Hospital, was astounded at what he heard on stage. "I couldn't believe this woman is really a physician," he said. "I felt she was dangerously misinformed."[24]

Reagan also appointed Dr. Frank Lilly, a Manhattan geneticist. Lilly was the first openly gay presidential appointee and much of the attention focused on his sexuality. At the meeting, Lilly was seated next to Cardinal John O'Connor, the archbishop of New York. The two chatted politely during the meeting while news cameras looked on. "I expect the cardinal and I will have some differences of opinion," Lilly said politely to reporters after the initial announcement. Some of Reagan's Capitol Hill allies pointedly criticized his naming Dr. Lilly to the commission. "The president should not be placing into positions of high visibility persons who are active and self-acknowledged homosexuals," said Senator Gordon Humphrey, a Republican from New Hampshire.[25] Ultimately, it was First Lady Nancy Reagan who insisted on the choice.[26]

Despite the Catholic Church's views on sex education, the church in New York had played a pivotal role in providing care to many AIDS patients. Cardinal O'Connor would remain mostly absent from the meetings, but when he was present, he surprised some of his fellow commissioners and staff. The Catholic Church opposed teaching about condoms or safe sex, but it still provided essential care to thousands of AIDS patients. The contradiction was difficult for some to understand, but the cardinal's appointment was more logical than just adding a religious figure to balance out others.

The panel's rocky start wasn't limited to the wild or inaccurate statements of its thirteen panelists. The committee quickly fell into greater turmoil when just three months after forming, the chairman and vice chairman resigned in frustration over the lack of progress and internal quarrels. The panel had also fired its executive director after three weeks. In an effort to dampen the chaos, President Reagan quickly appointed one of the remaining commissioners, retired Admiral James D. Watkins, to head up the effort.

Admiral Watkins spent thirty-seven years in the Navy serving as commander of the Sixth Fleet, vice chair of Naval Operations, commander-in-chief of the Pacific Fleet, and most recently as chief of Naval Operations. When asked to lead the group, Admiral Watkins told the president's team he knew little about medicine and epidemiology. But medicine was not the commission's main problem at that point. Someone needed to whip the panel into shape, and a retired admiral was just the right person for the task.

On his first day on the job, Admiral Watkins entered the commission's office in Washington, above Old Ebbitt Grill, one of Washington's oldest restaurants, to find it nearly empty. There was almost no staff to be found. Unopened mail was piling up on the desks, phones were laying on tables unplugged, and the government unit responsible for setting up the operation left a single tabletop copier for the staff to conduct their work. The panel had mere months to prepare a report to deliver to the president and there was little time to waste.

Admiral Watkins's first order of business garnered him early praise; he appointed two new commissioners with public health experience, both of whom had been critical of the Reagan administration's response. He made it clear to the president's team that he would make the decisions, not political staffers from their perches at the White House.

The commission's first preliminary report was released in February of 1988 and focused on how transmission related to IV drug use. Watkins wanted to release the report to give an early preview of things to come and show the commission was back on track. To the surprise of many, Admiral Watkins was very candid with his criticism of the federal response to the virus.

Pullen was focused on curbing IV drug use altogether. "This country has to come to grips with the root problem," she said during a hearing on drug use. She was not interested in quick fixes like intervention strategies.[27]

The panel's meetings were conducted like congressional hearings with the commissioners seated up high on a dais and witnesses providing opening statements and answering questions. The witnesses ran the gamut, from medical experts to everyday Americans affected by the virus. Ryan White, a student from Kokomo, Indiana, who had garnered national attention during his legal battle to return to his local public school, testified on two occasions. An older woman from California testified about how her husband contracted the virus through a blood transfusion, was diagnosed post-mortem, and had inadvertently spread it to her. On one occasion, a farmer from Iowa spoke about his difficult experience getting proper information on AIDS. "You know, the members of the gay Iowa farmers caucus are pretty few in number," he told the commissioners to laughter.[28]

On many occasions, the proceedings were picketed outside or interrupted inside by AIDS activists wanting to draw attention to the committee and hold them accountable. They came armed with chants and signs adorned with commissioners' names and faces, especially those like Penny

Pullen who they felt had no business being on the panel. One group in particular—ACT UP—could be found at nearly every gathering. Some commissioners and staff found the protests distracting and counterproductive, but those dying or seeing their friends pass away felt a sense of urgency as the numbers climbed. Pullen was used to being picketed when she attended events or seeing her name plastered on signs, and the attention did little to weaken her assurance that she was on the right path.

AIDS was a vicious virus that largely affected a single community. Because of this, many activists felt their concerns were being ignored nationally. If you opened up your average mainstream newspaper during the height of the AIDS crisis, you'd be hard-pressed to find many obituaries of men who had died. Flip to the obituary section of a gay newspaper in any major American city, however, and the contrast would be stunning. In Chicago's *Windy City Times*, the paper printed tributes each week to those who had passed. Like a sad song repeating a numb refrain, each listing followed a similar pattern. *John Smith passed away from AIDS-related complications on March 1, 1988.* Then followed the decedent's age, a number that in any other setting would be shocking to a reader. Here, it was par for the course. *He was twenty-five.* Or forty-one. Or just a few days shy of his thirtieth birthday. Surrounding each obituary were more obituaries, a constant reminder of the death looming around the paper's readers. AIDS wasn't just a story in the gay community, it was *the* story.

One activist who battled with Pullen in Illinois would later illustrate this mounting loss when recounting his attempt to throw a fiftieth birthday party for his partner. The couple had held a fortieth celebration just a decade earlier and enjoyed themselves immensely at the event. So, when they pulled out the guest list from the previous party to begin planning, they were dismayed to find out that of their 102 friends who last attended, more than half were now dead.[29] With stories like that in mind, activists had few qualms about making those in charge feel uncomfortable for a few moments.

After all the witnesses had spoken and the final site visits were conducted, the committee met on June 7, 1988, in Washington to discuss the final report. For over eight hours, Watkins and his staff led the committee chapter by chapter through the report, pausing to hear concerns from commissioners. They had just a few weeks left to deliver a report to the president and Watkins made it clear he was open to suggestions, but huge, wholesale changes to the document would be unwelcome.

The most contentious piece of the report was a recommendation for a federal nondiscrimination law for those suffering from AIDS. Supporters on the panel felt it would increase people's willingness to get tested if the threat of losing your job was eliminated. One of the panelists who was an oncologist, Dr. Burton Lee, spoke in favor of the measure and likened it to his experience with treating cancer patients. "One of the saddest things that I constantly have to face with practically all my patients is the discrimination that cancer patients get in the workplace. They are very, very commonly dropped from their jobs even when they're cured. So this is a statute that is close to my heart," he said.[30]

The conservatives on the panel disagreed. One worried aloud whether the measure would have political backlash in an election year. Watkins was stunned. He viewed the recommendation as critically important to the success of the report. "Bill, we're trying to do what we think is right here," he said in response to a commissioner's concerns.[31] He understood it would be viewed by the public as a giveaway to the gay community, but Watkins believed it was the right thing to do. His position had been solidified on the issue when hearing testimony at hearings about people who faced intense scrutiny once infected with the virus. He recounted one witness telling the commission about screams of "Kill him, kill him!" when parents at a school protested an AIDS-infected child's return. Because of this emotion, Watkins personally wrote the last chapter of the report.[32]

Every detail of the report had the potential to become a point of contention among the commissioners. Some commissioners worried about the language of "innocent" victims because they believed it implied others were guilty of something.[33] Toeing the line between providing sound public health advice and not upsetting the more puritanical panelists became a tightrope walk.

Pullen had concerns throughout the report about some of the language and the larger societal issues such as drug use and sex education. She sighed heavily into the microphone as she flipped through the pages with edits. "That's what I get for reading this thing," she said to her fellow commissioners during a final hearing.[34] Reading through chapters on testing and treatment, she requested paragraphs be moved up and down the pages. She moved commas and bullets. For Pullen, no detail was too small or inconsequential.

After months of meetings, twenty-three public hearings, and interviews with more than 550 witnesses, the commission finally released a final report in June of 1988. By then, about 64,000 Americans had been infected by the virus.[35] The report totaled 300 pages and had more than 600 recommendations for addressing the public health crisis. It advocated for $3 billion in additional funds to implement the recommendations and a federal nondiscrimination law to make sure testing was adequately ramped up. The report noted the importance of increased education about AIDS in health classes at the state level in schools, made it a crime to knowingly transmit the disease to others, and emphasized confidentiality in testing.

The opening pages began with a poem from the English poet John Donne: "No man is an Iland, intire of itselfe. . . . any mans death diminishes me, because I am involved in Mankinde."[36] It was an appeal to the humanity of everyone involved and a reminder to not let politics color the discussion of these recommendations. Despite the committee's rocky start, its work was praised by those who had doubted Watkins. He was able to build consensus among a very divided, political group of individuals. Even his harshest critics who were initially hesitant of the appointment were appreciative of his work.

News coverage focused particularly on the nondiscrimination piece. It was far more broadminded than anyone had anticipated, and the Reagan administration was caught off-guard by the recommendation.

Still, the response was largely positive. President Reagan lauded the work as an "impressive effort" but avoided discussing the antidiscrimination proposal.[37] The president accepted the report from Admiral Watkins during a fifteen-minute meeting in the Oval Office and handed the report over to his drug policy czar to formulate a plan within thirty days. In the end, many of the key recommendations remained untouched or were watered down. While mostly ignored by the administration, the report did provide a framework for federal agencies, lawmakers in Congress, and state leaders on various measures that could be taken to address AIDS. The final report was approved after fourteen hours of deliberation. The nondiscrimination recommendation was approved by a vote of 8 to 5. Pullen opposed.[38]

Reporters surround Penny Pullen at the state capitol in Springfield, Illinois, following a committee vote on her proposal to restrict abortion access after the United States Supreme Court's ruling in *Webster v. Reproductive Health Services*. Photo Credit: *Chicago Tribune*/TCA

4

Henry Penny

Welcome to this peaceful corner of the northwest suburbs, where the abortion battle rages a notch louder than in most of the rest of the state.

The home of Mary Reilly sat on a quiet corner of Seminary Avenue on the southwest side of suburban Park Ridge, Illinois. An ordinary neighborhood by most standards, her block was filled with tidy red-brick homes and lined with mature trees whose leaves were on the cusp of bursting into the radiant reds and golden yellows of autumn. Park Ridge was a slice of Americana, a place that sometimes felt like the living embodiment of a Norman Rockwell painting. It was the kind of town that was distant from the polarizing political battles of the day. At least for some residents.

Mary Reilly kept four large glass jars in her home. And inside the jars was not candy or flour, but fetuses. "This is what it's all about," she once told a reporter from the *Chicago Tribune* as she displayed her collection marking the various stages of pregnancy. The largest jar contained twenty-two-week twins which were given to her by the director of a closed nursing school in the area. One by one, she took each jar out of its box and placed it on her living room floor to help illustrate to the reporter her strong views on abortion. To her, the jars represented the barbarity of the Democratic party's stance on the issue. "Welcome to this peaceful corner of the northwest suburbs, where the abortion battle rages a notch louder than in most of the rest of the state," the *Tribune* piece began.[1]

Park Ridge had received a great deal of attention from activists on both sides of the abortion debate for a number of years. At the northernmost border of Park Ridge, Lutheran General Hospital, one of the largest hospitals in the Chicagoland area, implemented a new policy that allowed women to receive an abortion in the second trimester if their pregnancy revealed certain fetal abnormalities. To the distress of the hospital's leadership, Lutheran General's campus became ground zero in Illinois for prolife activists. Mary Reilly's jars would make an appearance at many rallies held on the sidewalk outside Lutheran General where fellow activists would use them as props on display for the media and passersby.

On the whole, Lutheran General's abortion policy wasn't that different from many of its peer hospitals in Illinois and across the country. It was, however, unique for a religiously affiliated institution, especially one that prominently displayed a cross on the top of its expansive facilities. Illinois hospitals overall tended to provide fewer abortion services, something many observers attributed to the strong Catholic influence of the Chicagoland community. Yes, this was a Lutheran hospital, but the public it served largely looked to the Vatican for guidance on this sensitive social issue.

In August of 1989, more than 250 protesters gathered at the hospital to show their anger over the policy. "How can we have a large and influential Christian hospital and health system that condones and participates in and justifies the killing of defenseless humans?" Reilly told reporters covering the event. Many of the demonstrators carried signs with slogans expressing their view that abortion was akin to murder. "Park Ridge murders babies," noted one poster held high for cars passing on the busy four-lane street between the hospital and a large, crowded strip mall.[2] Not far off in the distance, the shiny bleachers of Maine East High School's football field displayed a banner paying homage to the school mascot—the Blue Demons—which likely did not sit well with many of the protestors bearing crosses and signs emblazoned with verses from the Old Testament. Some of those demonstrating carried pictures of dead fetuses and handed out flyers to spectators with similar images, a pattern that repeated itself at prolife demonstrations across the country. In the protesters' view, they were merely showing just how repugnant they believed the procedures being performed in the hospital were, but their in-your-face tactics often turned off people who might otherwise be persuaded.

For two years, hospital officials had consulted with clergy, ethicists, doctors, and others to craft its first change to Lutheran General's abortion policy since 1974. But despite significant preparations, the hospital was still wading into one of the nation's hottest political issues. At one point during the demonstration, protesters threw blood on the sidewalk to illustrate their view that the hospital had blood on its own hands. No amount of preparation or measured consultations with community leaders would persuade activists otherwise.

Emotions ran hot in the local papers covering the activities around Lutheran General. Letters to the editor or opinion essays warned of "hanger back-alley abortions" if prolife activists ultimately had their way.[3] Some spoke graphically about such procedures and how they were conducted. Some women put their names on their letters and opinion pieces, while others used the local press as a chance to express their heartfelt beliefs on the issue anonymously. Many of the letters were deeply personal, more like notes to a friend than to their entire community. In a time before social media, a letter to the editor was one of the few ways to make your voice heard, and it took a lot more effort than clicking a button.

Penny Pullen, meanwhile, kept her work on the issue mostly behind the scenes. She was more likely to be found drafting legislation in Springfield than leading a picket line in Park Ridge. Still, she was ashamed that a hospital in her own backyard was out front on this issue and was happy to see she wasn't the only one taking notice.

For years, Pullen had worked on legislative topics that didn't involve abortion. Much of her work focused on correcting what she viewed as the ethical ills of society. As someone who attended college in the 1960s during the age of counterculture where antiwar protests dominated and Americans' attitudes toward many social norms relaxed, Pullen was struck by what she viewed as the slow but certain moral decay of American society. She viewed many of the defining events of the sixties as a backward slide for the country, a belief that informed much of where she devoted her time in the later decades.

As the American public began to wake up to the dangers of cigarettes, for instance, she worked to ban smoking in public schools. As some sectors of the country became enraged over a Supreme Court decision permitting the burning of the American flag as a protected expression of free speech, she pushed to make sure public school classrooms still began the day with a recitation of the Pledge of Allegiance, viewing it as a chance to solidify the patriotism of the country's youth. On taxes, she struck a shrewd deal with the governor, Republican "Big Jim Thompson," to repeal the state's inheritance tax. She knew the governor was facing one of the toughest political races of his life in 1982, and he would come to rely on the repeal of the inheritance tax to help bolster the support of Illinois farmers when he faced a challenge from Senator Adlai Stevenson III, who was particularly popular outside of Chicago. Thompson won that year by just 5,000 votes, and Pullen felt her legislation played a role in the victory.[4] Little by little, she was gaining clout in Springfield.

In her early days in the legislature, Pullen amassed a solidly conservative voting record. She voted against new regulations, shot down increased spending, and wasn't afraid to stand alone in opposing otherwise popular bills. She advanced into House leadership, dutifully supporting her caucus's agenda and taking tough votes when necessary. Sometimes that meant voting for bills she didn't support, like auto emissions testing for Illinois cars, which in her view was overly burdensome. When legislators put forth an income tax hike in 1983, she reluctantly voted for the increase because she thought it would stave off a larger one down the road.[5]

Going against certain matters of principle was agonizing for Pullen, and she knew difficult votes would have to be carefully justified to her constituents. But Pullen was comfortable enough in her seat to take the occasional political hit. She knew that after staking out a politically perilous position, she had the credibility to explain it away to constituents.

Pullen was constantly straddling the line between pragmatist and idealist, a challenge that many ambitious politicians face as they work to rise up the ranks. Casting a vote when the stakes are low is easy, but having to actually lead and help govern a caucus of lawmakers is a far more delicate task. This is part of the reason why when a new speaker of the House comes to power in Congress, they're quickly decried not just by their usual enemies, but by their most fervent partisans. An unfortunate side effect of the primary system nationwide is that it rewards politicians who serve merely as vacant vessels of the partisan will rather than effective and candid consensus-builders. Voters say they want compromise, but when compromise comes, those who dare cede ground are punished by strident party pushback. Pullen was somewhere in between, a politician with the sometimes contradictory goals of maintaining her status as an unshakeable conservative warrior while also managing to get something done.

Despite the challenge, Pullen indeed became known as someone who was able to achieve some legislative success on a variety of issues. But on no issue did she become better known than for her role as the most vocal pro-life leader in the state of Illinois. Nowhere was her commitment to the issue more evident than in her Park Ridge office, located in an upscale strip mall in the city's central shopping district that residents referred to as "Uptown."

Windows in Uptown displayed custom-tailored suits and the latest markdowns at Pine's of Park Ridge, a long-established men's clothing store with distinctive kelly-green signage at its corner location. Solari & Huntington, the local jeweler situated on Main Street, arranged its newest gold earrings and stylish wristwatches in shiny glass cases. Right next to the city's quaint, red-brick train station completed in 1960, the public library promoted upcoming community events—a board meeting, piano recitals, and a book club for young adults. In Pullen's office window, on the other hand, was an oversized picture of an eight-week-old fetus, something pedestrians passing by the nearby shops and restaurants could see from the sidewalk.[6]

The interior of Pullen's office made no secret of where her loyalties lay. Near her desk laid a decorative plate depicting Senator Barry Goldwater, for whom she had volunteered as a young high school Republican. On the wood-paneled walls of the office hung a signed picture of Ronald Reagan.[7] She was a big admirer of both Republican icons, but she was no acolyte blindly following along. Pullen was motivated by the *issues*, and the prolife cause was her guiding light.

Pullen was resolute in her position. She didn't believe in exceptions for rape, incest, or when the life of the mother was at risk. Exceptions were for squishes, she thought. Life begins at conception, full stop.[8] For her and others similarly like-minded, it was a matter of consistency. Why should a life produced from rape be held less valuable than one from a planned pregnancy? She made her view on this known in the legislature as well as back in the district. "I personally know a young woman who came from rape and I believe she has a right to life," she told a group of voters at a local Rotary Club meeting.[9] The woman's name was Julie Makimaa, another pro-life activist whom Pullen first met when Julie walked into her capitol office in Springfield to share her story. Julie's life encapsulated why, to Pullen, allowing for exceptions was a slippery slope.

Despite her inflexible views on abortion, Pullen was quite practical when it came to legislating on the issue. She was careful to pass measures that never went beyond the bounds of the law. Pullen genuinely wanted to impact change that would last, not throw proverbial red meat toward conservative constituents or idealistic activists that would likely be tossed out by the courts. When debating changes to a "waiting period" law that required women to wait a designated amount of time before being permitted to obtain an abortion, she amended the legislation to make it more likely to withstand judicial scrutiny by shortening the number of days a woman would be required to wait from twenty-four to twelve. Some of her prolife colleagues were confused at first when she proposed the change during a debate on the House floor. Pullen quickly assured them that this was more within the bounds of what courts would permit based on recent precedent. Knowing her to be the leader on this issue, her colleagues took her direction.[10] No one could doubt her intentions were sincere.

Pullen wasn't a lawyer, but she understood what it took to keep things in line with the law. She closely monitored what the courts said on the issues she cared about and attained a level of fluency with the legal jargon that many of her nonlawyer colleagues found perplexing. Each word and every piece of punctuation had meaning and purpose. In some years, every bill she sponsored that was sent over by her Senate colleagues she shepherded successfully through the House, garnering her praise from the *Chicago Tribune* as one of the legislature's "heavy hitters."[11] Pullen understood she was in the business of making laws, not bluster.

Like many in the prolife movement, Pullen's ultimate aspiration was for *Roe v. Wade* to be completely overturned and for the Supreme Court to reverse its earlier view that a woman has a right to privacy under the Fourteenth Amendment that includes whether or not to have an abortion. But that goal simply wasn't attainable from her perch in the legislature, so like many politicians over the years since *Roe*, she settled with merely chipping away at access to abortion over time. Little by little, the prolife movement would have its victories in the states and in the judiciary.

Detractors and supporters alike often compared Pullen to Republican congressman Henry Hyde, whose district overlapped with her own. The two politicians sometimes appeared together at events with local Republican organizations and community groups. One group of Pullen critics referred to her as "Henry Penny."[12] All in all, the comments comparing her to Hyde were a high compliment. He was the leader of the prolife movement in Congress, and any suggestion they were soldiers in the same battle was more than casual flattery. "She's not intimidated by anything. She's not a showboat. But her convictions are so strong that they carry her over any intimidation," Congressman Hyde noted about Pullen. "A lot of people don't like her because she's not a 'hail-fellow-well-met,' she's not a back-slapper. I know her as a full-steam-ahead engines-running-full kind of person," he said, noting that her strong convictions did not come packaged with the warm, disarming personality expected of most politicians.[13]

Henry Hyde was the namesake of the Hyde Amendment, which passed Congress in 1976 and prevents the use of federal funds to perform abortions. A former trial lawyer and Navy veteran, Hyde was raised as a New Deal Democrat. His bright white hair and wide frame made him stand out among a crowd of otherwise indistinguishable male colleagues. Hyde spoke calmly but with certainty, and he was never afraid of wading into a culture war with flare. "The only virtue to abortion is that it is a final solution," Hyde said on the floor of the House of Representatives in 1976, alluding not so subtly to Adolf Hitler and the Holocaust.[14]

In contrast to his firm opposition to abortion, Hyde sometimes bucked the party line on issues like gun control and, notably given his prolife views, family leave and federal assistance to low-income pregnant women and young children. He was a respected member during his time in the Republican conference and even some of his most ardent critics praised his consistency for supporting social programs designed to help women who would be required to carry a child instead of terminating a pregnancy because of the Hyde Amendment bearing his name. "He acted on the view that because he opposed abortion, that children would be born in difficult circumstances, and he felt an obligation to help them," the well-known liberal icon, Massachusetts congressman Barney Frank, would later note about his conservative colleague from Illinois.[15]

Until recent years, the Hyde Amendment was mostly uncontroversial. In 2016, the Democratic party added a repeal of the Hyde Amendment to its official platform. A strong supporter of the amendment as recently as 2019, President Joe Biden said during his 2020 campaign that he would work to repeal it. Supporters say the Hyde Amendment is merely commonsense; taxpayer money should not go toward something so many Americans deeply oppose. Those who advocate its repeal say it unfairly targets poor women who rely on Medicaid for health care and the amendment has a disparate impact on women of color. Still, every budget passed in Congress since 1976 has included this measure and any repeal would require Democrats to hold strong majorities in both the House and Senate.[16] Barring these changes, Henry Hyde's legacy lives on.

In 1989, Henry Hyde continued his work in Congress while Pullen pursued her own agenda in the Illinois House. That same year, the abortion debate raged anew when the United States Supreme Court announced it would hear oral arguments in *Webster v. Reproductive Health Services*. The case involved a Missouri law that implemented paralyzing restrictions on abortion clinics. The announcement gave prolife activists hope the nation's highest court would finally allow states to implement new restrictions and give a victory to the movement. From there, overturning *Roe*, they thought, would gain unstoppable momentum.

William Webster was the Missouri attorney general and plaintiff in the suit. He would go on to personally argue the case before the Supreme Court, something that is relatively rare for a state attorney general who typically hands the task off to professional staff, the state solicitor general, or outside counsel.[17] The case was important enough that the state's highest law enforcement officer wanted to be seen as the face defending it in court. It was a smart political move for someone harboring higher ambitions; successfully arguing for the overturn of *Roe* would make him an instant political hero on the right.

The Missouri law at issue in the *Webster* case said that unborn children had rights equal to full-grown adults. It forbade doctors employed or funded by the state government from performing abortions during pregnancies they deemed to be viable, and it said that public funds could not go toward encouraging women to get abortions. In sum, the statute introduced what many considered to be a radical legal position regarding the unborn and restricted access in a way most thought unconstitutional post-*Roe*. Some legal observers deemed it the "kitchen sink" law because drafters were throwing everything forward to see what would stick in the courts.[18] Prochoice activists worried aloud that this might be the case to finally overturn *Roe*.

The *Roe* decision had come down roughly fifteen years earlier and, in effect, legalized abortion nationwide. At the time, abortion was illegal in thirty states and legal in disparate forms in the rest. The case built its opinion around the privacy of individuals. The court said that a person, through the right to due process under the Fourteenth Amendment, has a right to privacy, and that includes a woman's decision whether to have an abortion. *Roe* was hailed by prochoice activists as a step toward reproductive freedom and criticized by opponents both for the impact it would have and the logic the court used to reach its 7–2 decision. In particular, conservatives believed the court was extending rights granted in the Fourteenth Amendment far beyond the bounds of its original intention.

A close watcher of the courts, Pullen decided to get moving on implementing a similar law to the one in Missouri while she waited for the Supreme Court to take up the issue. She wanted her state to be ready to go the moment, she hoped, the court pulled the proverbial trigger. In April of 1989, the same month the Supreme Court heard oral arguments on *Webster*, Pullen introduced a bill that would require a physician to determine whether a fetus could survive outside the womb before the abortion of a twenty-week-old. If a doctor deemed the fetus viable, a second doctor would be required to be on hand during an abortion in order to provide potential life support if the fetus survived. The changes she proposed made violating the law a felony for which a doctor could face up to ten years in prison. Any procedure had to be performed in a properly equipped hospital, not a clinic.[19]

The proposal wasn't a ban on abortion, but an obstacle that would be placed in the way of those seeking to perform or obtain one. "It is important, particularly for the best interest for the woman . . . that we limit the performance of such medical procedures to facilities where they can be properly cared for," Pullen said about her proposal, echoing a common argument from prolife activists that smaller abortion clinics were unsafe.[20] The law was emblematic of a back-and-forth that goes on between both sides whenever a new abortion law is proposed. Those who are prochoice assert these laws are dishonest and merely a ruse for outlawing abortion, while prolife legislators allege, mostly using legal reasons in order to withstand judicial scrutiny, that the regulations serve as necessary public health measures.

House Bill 574 became Pullen's opening salvo in what she thought was an imminent opportunity the Supreme Court would provide prolife lawmakers. She openly acknowledged her plan to legislate as far as the court would allow when speaking on the Illinois State House floor. "If the Supreme Court gives the states any more sovereignty or changes with what they have previously said with respect to abortion restrictions, then this bill would be a possible vehicle for that," she said, alluding to the impending *Webster* decision.[21] In Pullen's words, she was ready to "walk through the window the Supreme Court has opened."[22]

This wasn't her first attempt at legislating on abortion, and Pullen had done much more than give speeches on the issue. Years earlier, she supported a bill that would include harsher penalties for an individual who commits manslaughter or murder against a pregnant woman. She had received a letter from the father of a woman who was killed in a drunk driving accident eight-months pregnant. Both the baby and the mother died, and Pullen wanted to ensure the fetus in the womb was counted as a separate human in these rare instances. Some prochoice legislators voted against the measure because it defined life as beginning at conception, and they viewed it as a back door challenge to *Roe*. As they saw it, the measure wasn't about harsher penalties for crimes; it was a springboard that could serve as a pretext for outlawing abortion.[23] In another bill, Pullen sought to create a law that would allow men to seek a court injunction to prevent a woman they had impregnated from having an abortion. Pullen said it was merely intended to give fathers a say in the process, while critics alleged the law would potentially prevent rape victims from terminating a pregnancy, a critique Pullen found completely detached from reality.[24]

There are generally two types of bills introduced in legislatures across the country. The first type is one of substance. It's the kind of bill that a legislator hopes to pass by scrounging up enough votes to get the measure out of committee, advance it to a full floor vote, garner approval from the other legislative body, then send it to the executive for signature giving the idea full force of law. There are also messaging bills. These bills are introduced by legislators not to make a difference or become law, but because they want to send a signal to constituents or activists that they are fighting for what these groups believe. Such bills are designed at getting media attention. But Pullen wasn't interested in sending signals, and messaging bills were never her cup of tea. Ever the realist, Pullen eventually pulled the fetal viability bill so she could wait until the Supreme Court ruled that summer in *Webster* and she had more direction on what might be permitted. She hoped the court would overturn *Roe* altogether, but it appeared more likely the justices would instead deal the precedent a death by many cuts. Pullen prayed this would be the first stab.

Years earlier when Justice Potter Stewart announced his retirement from the United States Supreme Court in 1981, most legal observers thought President Reagan would use the vacancy as a chance to fulfill his campaign promise of appointing a woman to the bench. During the 1980 campaign, Reagan had been running a large approval deficit with women and the campaign worried about his ability to cross the finish line without the support of more female voters. "It is time for a woman to sit among our highest jurists," he had said during a news conference, seeking to deliver a symbolic victory for half the voting population.[25] Whether a self-serving political move or a sincere nod to gender parity, it helped distract from criticism he faced for opposing the Equal Rights Amendment in the final stretch of the campaign. Decades later, Joe Biden would offer a similar pledge in 2020 by vowing to appoint a Black woman to the Supreme Court, a promise he would eventually fulfill with Justice Ketanji Brown Jackson's successful appointment to the bench. History shows us, it appears, that despite assertions otherwise, both sides of the aisle engage in identity politics when it serves to benefit them politically.

When President Reagan announced his decision in 1981 to appoint an Arizona Court of Appeals judge named Sandra Day O'Connor, many conservatives were skeptical. O'Connor's record on abortion was unclear at best. She hadn't ruled on any cases relevant to the matter as a judge, but as a member of the Arizona State Senate she had voted against a few measures that would have fully criminalized abortion. If anything, her scant record suggested her to be a moderate, and that simply wasn't good enough for some purists. A few of O'Connor's votes, in fact, were missing in the record on various abortion-related measures when researchers went to dig them up at the Arizona Legislature.[26] Critics felt that if confirmed, she would not go far enough in moving the court toward overturning *Roe*. Pullen, being one of them, wrote President Reagan a letter criticizing his administration for potentially abandoning conservatives.

In the letter, Pullen referenced her trepidation about O'Connor's abortion views and also chastised Reagan's team for leading him astray. She felt some staff and cabinet members were not true conservatives. In particular, she believed Secretary of State George Schultz was a weak leader on the national stage more interested in his own agenda than fulfilling the promises Reagan had laid out on the campaign trail.

Reagan felt a need to respond to Pullen. After returning to the White House on August 30, 1981, from a vacation at his California ranch, the president began catching up on correspondence by dictating letters into his

Norelco mini-cassette player. He dictated a letter to conservative thought leader William F. Buckley to wish him recovery from a recent foot injury. He dictated a letter to Freeman Gosden, a radio personality and minstrel actor well known for his work with the *Amos 'n' Andy* show, thanking him for sending a gift to the White House and telling him it was nice to see him at a recent dinner party. But before that, he dictated a reply to Penny Pullen. "Dear Representative Pullen, I received your letter of August 24th and appreciate very much your giving me the chance to comment on the situation," the president said, with the faint pattering of a fan oscillating audibly in the background. "Let me first, however, thank you very much for all the help you've given me on the campaign and for your support since 1964." Then he directly addressed her alarm about Sandra Day O'Connor:

> I understand your concern about the court appointment, but please, I ask you to believe, that I feel as deeply as you do about the issue of abortion. I have not weakened in my belief that the interrupting of a pregnancy means the taking of a human life. . . . I gave a great deal of study before appointing Judge O'Connor. I am confident I made the right decision. As I said before, if I should be proven wrong, then the mistake is mine. Feeling as strongly as I do on the issue of abortion, does it seem likely that I would have been careless about this appointment? I appreciate very much your saying that in spite of this you would continue to support me. I hope you will have no reason to regret this . . . best regards, sincerely, Ronald Reagan.[27]

Sandra Day O'Connor went on to be confirmed 99–0 in the United States Senate, a number that would be unheard of in a twenty-first-century confirmation. But for most of the court's history, this kind of consensus was all but presumed. Still, O'Connor's record over the next few decades would mostly prove conservatives right on their early suspicions. As the so-called swing vote on many issues during her tenure, she became known for her practical, middle-of-the-road approaches to many legal issues and penchant for balancing tests.

One of the first abortion cases O'Connor would have a say in was *Webster* and on July 3, 1989, the Supreme Court released its much-anticipated decision. It was a stark blow for the prochoice movement and a first crack in the foundation of *Roe*. The court said in a 5–4 decision that the Missouri statute at issue was mostly permitted under law, but the justices refused to consider the constitutionality of *Roe*. Still, their decision would pave the way for legislatures to further restrict access to abortion across the country.

"Nothing in the Constitution requires States to enter or remain in the business of performing abortions," Chief Justice William Rehnquist wrote for the majority. Aside from the holding itself, much of the attention focused on the concurring opinions of the other justices who agreed with the outcome but for different reasons. Justice O'Connor agreed with the majority and refused to go along with some of her conservative colleagues in overturning *Roe* outright, writing that "there is no necessity to accept the State's invitation to reexamine the constitutional validity of *Roe v. Wade.*" In her eyes, the Missouri law and *Roe's* protection of privacy under the Fourteenth Amendment were two separate issues. A time would come when it was appropriate for a full evaluation of the court's precedent, but this was not it.

Justice Antonin Scalia, one of the conservative movement's judicial lodestars, scolded Justice O'Connor in his separate concurring opinion. Both agreed that the law was constitutional, but Scalia found his colleague's reticence to fully address *Roe* cowardly. Her view on exercising judicial restraint "cannot be taken seriously," he wrote. Scalia worried about the court appearing political by avoiding the issue because of public pressure. "We can now look forward to at least another Term with carts full of mail from the public, and streets full of demonstrators, urging us—their unelected and life-tenured judges who have been awarded those extraordinary, undemocratic characteristics precisely in order that we might follow the law despite the popular will—to follow the popular will," he wrote, accusing her of bowing to political pressure.[28]

Indeed, Scalia was correct about the continued political pressure that would result. Prolife groups continued to rally in Washington each year as they had since 1974 for the March for Life. The event marked the anniversary of *Roe v. Wade,* and the crowds grew bigger over time. On the pro-choice side, nearly 300,000 people had gathered in Washington in April of 1989 in advance of oral arguments for *Webster.* "It is a statement to the political leadership of this country—to President Bush, the Congress of the United States and the Supreme Court—that the women of this country will not go back. There is no turning back for us," said Molly Yard, president of the National Organization for Women at the Washington rally. Prolife groups made their opposition known to the marchers by placing 4,400 white crosses and stars of David on the West Front of the Capitol in what they declared a "Cemetery of the Innocents."[29] If there was one thing prolife groups remained skilled at, it was grabbing attention.

Reaction to the *Webster* decision was quick from both ends. Scalia's criticism of O'Connor paralleled Pullen's and many conservatives' earlier concerns upon her appointment. When asked for her view on the decision, Pullen echoed the general feeling among prolife leaders. "It's a step in the right direction, but I wanted the *Roe v. Wade* ruling overturned . . . I wanted the Supreme Court to say their 1973 ruling was wrong," she said.[30] Pressed further about the impact it could have on abortion laws nationwide, she didn't mince words. "I don't believe in genocide," she replied in a clear swat at prochoice advocates who thought the decision's upholding of the law was improper. When asked about how *Webster* might affect women in Illinois, her response was equally sharp. "I don't deal with women who have abortions, so I don't know how many it will affect," she said.[31] One constituent called Pullen's comments "Hitlerian."[32] But those reactions didn't concern Pullen very much. The Supreme Court announced its decision on a Monday, and by Tuesday legislators were already moving. Pullen began drafting a bill mirroring the Missouri law the court had just upheld. Her quick work was illustrative of a chain reaction that is commonly set off following Supreme Court decisions. When the nation's highest court signals there is room to move on a particular issue, it typically falls to the state legislatures to take the first steps.

Back in her district, the *Webster* decision reverberated at Lutheran General Hospital. Officials there weren't quite certain how the new ruling would impact their abortion policy, and the announcement put them back in the crosshairs of local activists. "It's still very early," a Lutheran General spokeswoman said. "It looks as if they're throwing the decision back to the states. We're just going to have to wait and see what action the state [will] take."[33] Just a few weeks later, another protest at the hospital was announced for that September. Both sides were energized by the ruling, and the otherwise unassuming suburban hospital again became the center of attention for prolife demonstrators. The fourth demonstration that year attracted more than 700 people. For more than two hours, supporters marched across the hospital's sidewalk chanting and passing out flyers. There was a renewed sense of hope among the crowd that the court's recent ruling might, this time, force Lutheran General to change its abortion policy.

Despite Pullen's status as one of the leaders of the prolife movement in Illinois, the issue of abortion had rarely been discussed in her previous election campaigns. Pullen ran on straight-ahead, bread-and-butter Republican issues: property taxes, supporting the local schools, and ensuring that the state got its fiscal house in order. Campaigning on social issues like abortion simply wasn't part of her approach. That would soon change.

With a new bill—a draft almost identical to the Missouri law upheld by the Supreme Court in *Webster*—Pullen got to organizing its introduction before the Illinois State House Rules Committee in October of 1989 during a two-week special session. She would need to convince her fellow committee members that this bill should be advanced through a rarely used emergency procedure, which was required of measures moving through the special session. The committee had seventeen members and ten votes were required to advance a bill.

Unlike today's politics where party is a clear indication of stance on abortion, the politics of the issue were much less rigid in 1989. The committee was made up of ten Democrats and seven Republicans. Pullen expected to have the support of six Republicans and at least three Democrats; only one vote would be needed for her to move forward. For Pullen, there was no greater emergency than putting an end to abortion as swiftly as possible. Given the committee had recently deemed a riverboat casino licensing measure to be an "emergency," she felt this was a no-brainer. And post-*Webster*, she wanted Illinois to be one of the first states to act.

At a rally before the hearing with the House Rules Committee, more than 400 people gathered to support the measure, waving handwritten signs with messages like "Thank you Penny Pullen—from unborn fetuses." Supporters exulted. "She is not a political chameleon—thank God for Penny Pullen," one Park Ridge constituent who came to support her battle enthusiastically proclaimed. Pullen was comforted to see many local constituents cheering her on, sharing her beliefs and willing to drive the three hours to Springfield to show their support.[34] On the capitol steps, speakers encouraged those gathered to lobby their legislators "until they're sick of your face."[35]

Overlooking the crowd was the zinc-topped dome of the Illinois Capitol, which towers above the rest of the city. Springfield, the city where a young Abraham Lincoln got his start, is full of symbols—bronze statues of statesmen, the corner law firm where the future president sharpened his legal mind, and the historic Old State Capitol building that served as the stage for his famed "House Divided" speech. The prolife movement understood the power of symbols too, and just a few feet from the podium, an empty, white, baby-sized casket stood on display. The governor had also recently vetoed another bill that would have banned the use of fetal tissue for medical experimentation in research for diseases like Parkinson's and Alzheimer's. The demonstrators were appalled that the governor's actions would allow stem cells to be used for this kind of research. "We need to tell Governor Thompson that we won't stand for little babies being killed so that their tissue can be used," Pullen told the cheering crowd.[36]

After the rally, Pullen gathered witnesses to address the House Rules Committee, a room with floor-length red curtains fit for a movie premiere, a staggered dais where the members sat overlooking the audience, and the great seal of Illinois, with an eagle's wings spread wide, looming above it all. Before an audience packed with TV cameras and reporters, extensive and emotional testimony was heard from both sides, each exhausting their usual arguments in the somber, courtroom-like atmosphere. Then, the time finally came for a vote, with ten votes necessary to advance the bill to the full House floor. "There are actually individuals present in their mother's wombs whose lives will depend on the votes we cast today," Pullen warned her colleagues while she gripped the microphone from her seat on the committee's dais.[37] Dressed in a white blouse with a plum-colored jacket, she wore a pearl necklace and dark red lipstick. "Vote 'aye' for life," she implored her colleagues in one final plea, leaning into the microphone.[38] As voting began, the crowd gathered inside looked on closely with anticipation, counting each "aye" as the legislators went down the roll call. Ultimately, the bill failed to advance from committee because of a single Republican legislator from suburban Elmhurst, just outside of Chicago, who said the measure was "bad public policy." The final tally was 9–8.[39]

Pullen exited the committee room as fourteen TV cameras, innumerable radio microphones, and reporters with tape recorders from around the country swarmed her. Post-*Webster*, Illinois was one of the first states to act and she was at the center of it all. The loss was a crushing personal setback, a glory moment gone wrong. Furious at her colleagues, Pullen let loose. "There's a lot of blood on the heads of some of the people in that room today, and I hope they really give it some reconsideration," she said with a cluster of microphones shoved inches from her face, clearly enraged at her fellow legislators.[40] She was particularly upset at the Democratic speaker of the House who, as a devout Catholic, professed to share her views on abortion but had deferred to the differing views of his caucus.

Choking back her dismay, Pullen knew this was the most urgent matter the House would take up this session. Taxes, flooding, and schools were all important, but there was nothing more urgent in her view than the opportunity to protect unborn human life. She reinforced that view for the cameras by wearing a gold lapel pin shaped like two baby feet representing the prolife movement. With Pullen's bill failing to advance out of committee, she would not have another opportunity to move her legislation forward until next spring when the legislature returned to session. She believed this was far from the end of the road.

As the political furor over the *Webster* decision grew and states across the country began working to restrict abortion, prochoice activists also looked ahead, setting their sights on the next election. They knew that if the courts wouldn't protect abortion rights, it was up to them to make sure elected officials did so. But they needed a test case, someone to target and send a message nationwide that restricting abortion would spell electoral trouble. Illinois, with one of the earliest primaries in the nation set to take place in March of 1990, would be the first battleground. Locals began to take notice too. "It's distressing that so far nobody has found the wherewithal to run against her," said a Park Ridge voter when asked by the *Chicago Sun-Times* about Penny Pullen's abortion fight. "I wish somebody would find it."

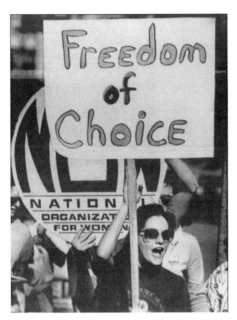 

Left: A prochoice demonstrator marches through downtown Park Ridge following a rally on October 15, 1989. Those gathered came to voice their opposition any changes to Illinois abortion laws following the Supreme Court's *Webster* ruling.
Right: From across the street, a group of prolife counterdemonstrators voice their opposition to the event. Photo Credit: *Pioneer Press*/TCA

Two Cents

For two cents, I'd do that!

Running late had become a habit for Rosemary Mulligan. She was known for being straightforward, one might say blunt, and never shying away from expressing her true feelings. Mulligan was the kind of person you could trust to always tell you the truth. You could not trust, however, that she'd be on time.

At forty-eight, Mulligan also took her appearance seriously. She wasn't a narcissist about her looks, but she understood it was important to don a little makeup, press her clothes before putting them on, and always make sure her strawberry blonde hair was in order. Presentation mattered. On this day in particular, she knew people would be paying attention.

It was a Sunday, and Mulligan was set to speak at a political rally in neighboring Park Ridge. The forecast foretold an uncharacteristically hot October 1989 day, with temperatures rising in the 80s. It was also an uncharacteristic event for Mulligan. Although she had been involved in local politics here and there, she was certainly no political activist. In fact, when a partner at the law firm where she worked ran for a state legislative seat just a few years prior, Mulligan had not been particularly engaged. She was busy raising a family, settling into her new career, and focusing on all the challenges life had thrown at her.

When Mulligan received a call from a leader from the local National Organization for Women chapter inquiring if she would speak at a pro-choice rally in Park Ridge, she jumped at the chance. By 1989, Mulligan had been a twenty-four-year resident of the area, and she felt drawn to be further engaged in politics. Both of her sons were grown and the younger,

Matt, was midway through college just three hours away at the University of Illinois. With her mother having died just a few months earlier, the rally provided Mulligan a welcomed distraction from mourning the loss of her namesake.[1]

A few years into her career as a paralegal, Mulligan had become involved with women's organizations such as her local chapter of the Illinois Business and Professional Women (BPW). The group was politically engaged both in Springfield and on the local level. It was made up of working women from all career paths and was thought of by some as a more moderate counterpart to the National Organization for Women. Mulligan's politics were ever so slightly to the right, and the group offered a chance for her to be engaged and learn more about things happening at the state capitol in Springfield. Despite her views on some issues, Mulligan defied party orthodoxy on issues like the Equal Rights Amendment. Abortion, in particular, was a motivating issue for Mulligan and she was adamant about her prochoice views. She believed it was none of the government's business to tell women what to do medically, and she thought being prolife was inconsistent with the traditional small-government views ascribed to by Republicans like herself.

From time to time, Mulligan would help organize support from her BPW chapter on issues before the legislature and lobby policymakers on the problems affecting the association's members. In time, she crafted a reputation as a sort of Republican spokesperson for the group, someone able to bridge the party gap where others could not. In this sense, she was an important voice for the rally organizers.

When Mulligan arrived at the park where the rally was to be held around 1 p.m., cars packed the street. The staging area was set up between Park Ridge's colonial-style city hall, the Uptown business district made up of mostly small boutique stores and restaurants, and the city's oldest church, a simple but distinct brick building built in 1877 with Gregorian-style symmetry and a white bell tower overlooking the triangle-shaped park. Around 200 supporters—mostly women—had gathered in the tree-lined park to hear speakers talk about impending changes that would be coming post-*Webster* if they didn't organize and stop the legislature from acting in Springfield. Mulligan, like most of the women gathered, was angered by the Supreme Court's willingness to extend states more latitude in restricting abortion. The ruling created an opening for state legislators who opposed abortion to act with newfound freedom on the issue, a reality that caused panic and a sense of urgency among those gathered in the park.

Mulligan was slated to speak along with the local NOW chapter president Ellen Yearwood, elected officials, and leaders from prochoice groups such as the Illinois Pro-Choice Alliance and Chicago Abortion Fund. She was used to speaking with elected officials or their staffs when working on behalf of the Business and Professional Women, but speaking at a full-fledged political rally was a new experience for her.

Also among the speakers was an ob/gyn who performed abortions for women in Chicago, a person who critics deemed an "abortionist." For groups on both sides of the debate nationwide, this is just a small example of how language serves as an important and powerful tool for persuasion, a never-ending opportunity to reframe words and make them more favorable to your side. *Prochoice* or *prolife. Fetus* or *unborn child. Medical doctor* or *abortionist.* Abortion is one of the few issues in politics where you can immediately guess a person's view just by hearing the vernacular they use when discussing it. The Park Ridge rally organizers understood, however, that the only language that mattered now was the language being written into proposed legislation before the General Assembly.

The event was being held just before the beginning of the Illinois General Assembly's annual "veto" session where a new law mirroring the Missouri statute upheld in *Webster* was likely to be introduced. This annual session provided legislators an opportunity to review old bills that might have been rejected by the governor and also a chance to introduce last-minute, emergency bills. Some of the rallygoers announced their intention of heading to Springfield after the rally to show their opposition and lobby legislators. At the same time President George H. W. Bush vetoed a bill that would have permitted Medicaid funds to be used for abortion in the cases of rape and incest, a move that would only incite the passion of prochoice activists even further.

Surrounding the park were roughly twenty counterdemonstrators who came to show their disgust for the prochoice gatherers. They lined their cars on the street surrounding the park and adorned them with large posters crafted with pictures and slogans about abortion. A white van stood near the counterdemonstrators with a "Stop Abortion Now" banner and an enlarged picture of a fetus hanging overhead. Others held red stop sign—shaped posters with slogans like "Abortion: an American holocaust" and "Latin translation for fetus is 'little one,' not trash."[2]

None of the reaction from the other side surprised the organizers. The groups planning this march had previously held a similar demonstration just a year earlier. They received a decent turnout in 1988, but prochoice voters were now paying much closer attention to the issue this year and *Webster* provided an easy recruiting tool.

At the previous rally, prolife demonstrators clashed with the organizers, trying to disrupt their plans. What started as a simple gathering in quiet, quaint Park Ridge quickly morphed into a raucous struggle between two groups of equally passionate advocates for their cause.

In a show of force, the prolife demonstrators had formed a line preventing the march from going forward through the city's downtown area. Many of these same people had been protesting at Lutheran General Hospital for years. The prochoice activists had considered demonstrating outside the hospital to show support for the institution's abortion policy, but they decided it was better not to direct more attention to an already volatile situation. Now, they had no choice but to face down their political foils.

Fed up with the antics and unproductive shouting from both sides on the protest line, a group of women turned around and marched just a few yards away to the steps of the Park Ridge police station. The women chanted outside of the building demanding a response from law enforcement. They were asking the police to remove the agitators and allow them to press forward with the march. Finally, officers agreed to escort the prochoice group through the downtown area and let them finish as planned. For a sleepy suburb whose police force was mostly accustomed to writing traffic tickets and arresting drunk high schoolers, the rally provided quite a challenge.

This year, the organizers were taking no chances. About a dozen police officers were dispatched to protect the group as they marched. Rallygoers were instructed to simply ignore any antagonism from the other side. And luckily this time around, the prolife demonstrators did not bring bull horns to disrupt the speeches. The mood of the rally was much calmer, and even the weather stood in contrast to the previous gathering. Rallygoers in 1988 brought jackets and umbrellas as they walked on a frigid, rainy day. Today was a sunny change of pace. "The difference a year makes," remarked a headline in the *Park Ridge Advocate*.[3]

Organizers firmly insisted this was not an anti—Penny Pullen demonstration. It was about showing the community there was a movement afoot in support of abortion rights. Despite that insistence, however, the intention was quite clear. Even the notices in the paper of the rally warned Pullen and other elected officials that they were "not representing their district when they sponsor/support anti-abortion legislation."[4] Speakers echoed this warning too. "Penny Pullen and her ilk are anti-women," one of the first speakers said to loud boos. The mere mention of Pullen's named evoked a strong reaction from the crowd. "Dump Penny Pullen!" the speaker finished to cheers. "We're going to need strength and endurance to put abortion rights back on track in this country," declared another speaker, the leader of Illinois's National Abortion Rights Action League chapter.[5]

When Mulligan spoke, she described her experience meeting with legislators and talked about the need for women to engage. She had a certain shakiness to her voice, but her views were firm, and she spoke from a place of deep belief. The crowd was receptive to her speech, and Mulligan was encouraged by the show of support. For years, she thought voters in the 55th state legislative district were more prochoice than the ideologies of the legislators representing them would suggest. It was a Republican area, yes, but Mulligan believed the likes of Penny Pullen and Henry Hyde were extreme. The suburban surroundings and midwestern modesty of local voters meant, in her view, people would rather not be represented by controversial figures, even if they agreed privately with their more provocative statements.

As other women went up on stage to make their speeches, a person from the crowd yelled, "One of you has to step up and beat Penny Pullen!"[6] The crowd roared in agreement, and Mulligan could sense the nerve-wracking feeling of eyes turning to her in that moment, not so subtly suggesting she be the one to heed the call. She continued listening to the speeches and applauded in agreement with the rest of the rallygoers.

When the main organizer of the rally had called Mulligan weeks earlier and invited her to speak, they had also discussed a potential challenge to Penny Pullen in the Republican primary. Mulligan was intrigued and open to the idea, but she wasn't entirely sure how difficult it would be to take out a fourteen-year incumbent, let alone one who was in Republican leadership in the House and had a national following. But like many of the people gathered at the rally that day, Mulligan disdained Pullen, and the thought of going up against someone she believed was a bigot was at least worth considering. The strong showing at the rally certainly helped her feel there might be enough support for a potential challenge.

As the rally went on, counterprotesters continued to yell from afar as speakers presented their case on stage. "Baby killers, go home!" they shouted over and over in an attempt to drown them out.[7] During one speech, two men ran next to a car parked behind the stage. They climbed on top of the vehicle and unfurled an oversized color poster depicting two aborted fetuses and lifted it up to face the prochoice rallygoers gathered in the park. The men were met with jeers. Without hesitation, some rally organizers ran toward the graphic sign and covered it while police removed the men from the park.

As Bonnie Lindquist, one of the local township trustees, gave her speech at the podium, a heckler from among the crowd began to yell and interrupt her. He shouted as she continued while he was removed from the park, this time by volunteer escorts. The rally organizers used volunteer escorts who were trained to help guide women entering abortion clinics past crowds of protesters. In other words, they were used to this sort of confrontation. When the man returned to the other side of the street and regrouped with his prolife compatriots, he began to shout again. "Let's hear it for Penny Pullen!" he said to cheers from his like-minded protestors.[8]

As the speeches finished, the prochoice demonstrators gathered with their banners and prepared to march through the downtown area. Mulligan grabbed a banner along with the head of the local NOW chapter and began leading marchers down the street. They chanted and waved their signs as police officers escorted them through the city center. Mulligan donned a lapel pin in support of the cause and waved to bystanders along the way. She sported large jet-black sunglasses on her face to block out the unseasonably blistering sun. For Mulligan, it was an enthralling and cathartic experience to see such strong support in an otherwise conservative area.

When the march ended, some of Mulligan's fellow rallygoers decided to go for coffee at the Pickwick Restaurant, a local diner just walking distance from the park on the corner of two busy streets at the center of town. The diner was a mainstay of the area and sat right next to the city's historic Pickwick Theater, one of last remaining movie palaces in operation that harkened back to an era of opulent cinemas once ubiquitous to Chicagoland. Built in 1928, the Art Deco style building soared over the rest of the city and became a symbol of the community.

The women were exhilarated from the march as they entered the diner and found a place to sit. They felt with enough momentum they could prevent any serious advancement of abortion legislation through the General Assembly in Springfield this session. But even more than any bills passing through the legislature, the women were focused on Penny Pullen. They were outraged that their own legislator was the one leading the prolife movement in Illinois. Others thought she was simply out of touch. Some of the sentiments the women expressed about Pullen were, put simply, less diplomatic.

As the women sipped their coffee from sturdy ceramic mugs sitting in red-cushioned booths, they talked about Pullen's record on abortion, AIDS, and the Equal Rights Amendment. They also discussed how she seemed to vote no on every piece of legislation they supported and she often stood alone in doing so. Eventually, the conversation turned to who might be up to the job of challenging Pullen, and the women again turned to Rosemary Mulligan.

Mulligan knew the conversation was already happening behind her back as people began to put her name forward. They knew she certainly wasn't shy about expressing her views given she had agreed to speak at the rally. They also knew Mulligan was a Republican, unlike many of the rally organizers, and given the political makeup of the district, Pullen could only be taken out in a primary. But even Mulligan wasn't sure if defeating Pullen would be possible. Still, she felt heartened by her friends' offer of help and knew there was a pressing need. "We'll help you!" they insisted, nudging her along.[9]

At the very least, Mulligan thought, running for public office might provide her a learning opportunity that she could take back to her Business and Professional Women chapter and, even as a losing candidate, counsel others about how to run for office or hold workshops for prospective candidates. She felt it would be worth the time and putting up an energetic fight, even in defeat, would put Pullen on notice.

Mulligan turned to her friends and cracked a joke about what it would take for her to run. "For two cents, I'd do that!" she quipped.[10] Mulligan was energized. She had nothing to lose. One of the women dug into her purse and pulled out two pennies and handed them to Mulligan. "Here's two cents. Run!" she said to laughter.[11] The race was on.

Campaign co-chair Diddy Blythe (left) and candidate Rosemary Mulligan in her second-floor campaign office in 1990. Photo Credit: *Daily Herald*

6

On the Trail

We're going to pretend we never took this poll and we're not going to tell Rosemary.

For many local candidates, deciding to run for the state legislature may seem at first like aspiring to just a step above the high school student council. Candidates are often convinced they will be able to sway any on-the-fence voter to their viewpoint if they can just look them in the eyes and have a civil conversation. Quickly, those early notions that everyone will give them a fair shake are shattered.

When a bright-eyed hometown candidate announces, he or she begins to be perceived differently. Neighbors who send their kids to school alongside yours suddenly view you with suspicion. After advertisements hit mailboxes and your picture appears in the paper, strangers do double-takes as you pass them in the grocery store, a constant reminder that your previously unappreciated privilege of anonymity is now shattered. Before someone shakes your hand, chances are they've already formed an opinion about you based on what they've read in the paper. And if you're elected, people come out of the woodwork to ask for favors. A deadbeat cousin who *definitely* deserves a state job. A tax benefit that's about to expire but most certainly merits renewal. An assist with an issue that has absolutely nothing to do with state government, but the clueless beggar knows not the wiser.

No matter how prepared a person might feel, the experience of being a candidate can only be fully understood by those who have put themselves forward. Only those who've subjected themselves to open and public judgment by their friends and neighbors can grasp what it truly means to have your name on the ballot. Above all, it requires a certain level of comfort with the possibility that your candidacy may result in a public humiliation in front of nearly everyone you know.

For Mulligan, it was clear from the beginning this campaign would be emotion-filled at every turn, and the local coverage of the prochoice rally was an early indication. Newspapers in the area were flush with letters to the editor, and many residents didn't hold back. "There is legislation now before our state legislature which will return us back to the dark ages, courtesy of Penny Pullen," wrote Geraldine Tarbutton, a local prochoice voter who expressed frustration the rally hadn't been better attended. She went on to share her own intimate story with the entire city. "Two years ago, my amniocentesis came back with the results of a Down's Syndrome baby. Making such a decision was not an easy one (as so many pro-lifers make it out), but it was one that had to be made. Luckily with me, I was able, with my doctor, to make a choice," she wrote. She then talked about her own experience demonstrating at the event in Park Ridge. "Being at the rally was painful and difficult for me, but it had to be done, so that other women in America and Illinois will also have the freedom of choice. When I saw those pro-lifers who taunted and harassed those at the rally, I knew they had no idea how much pain some of us have gone through."[1]

As always, there were letters on the other side too. One prolife woman penned a note about the regret she felt for having an abortion early on in her life. "Had I known one brave nurse who would've explained to me that in a saline abortion the only skin not burned and red is the palm and that skin is only spared because the tiny life therein clenched its fist in pain and terror," she wrote in a somewhat stream-of-conscience fashion describing a now rare but much-criticized procedure where saline solution is injected into the uterus to burn the fetus.[2] The writer left her name off the piece, but expressed support for the *Webster*-style changes that Pullen was pushing through the legislature.

Despite her gung-ho discussion with friends after the rally, Mulligan ultimately didn't make a full commitment to running until her hand was somewhat forced. One of the women she was drinking coffee with at the Pickwick Restaurant after the rally promptly leaked her deliberations to a local paper. When she received a call from a reporter, Mulligan explained that she thought Pullen was out of touch with her constituents and someone needed to challenge her.

When the article came out, it appeared the choice had officially been made. "Pro Choice Republican to Challenge Pullen," the headline in the *Park Ridge Herald* read in late November 1989. The ink was dry, and the paper was already landing on doorsteps across the district. There was no going back. And with just barely four months until the March 20 primary election, there was little time to spare.

Mulligan's son Matt was in his sophomore year at the University of Illinois Urbana-Champaign when she called him up to tell him the news. She had been increasingly engaged in politics through her various associations and volunteer groups, but the announcement still came as somewhat of a surprise to some of the family. Still, most of them were supportive of the effort. When Mulligan married into her first husband's family, she was surrounded by local politics. Her father-in-law and brother-in-law became alderman on the Des Plaines city council and were loyal Republicans, volunteering for the local organization and remaining engaged where they could. But small, nonpartisan city council races like those would pale in comparison to the preparations needed to mount a proper run for state representative. The people whose votes she would be courting extended far beyond the comfortable confines of her neighborhood.

Staring into the abyss of the early days of a political campaign in November of 1989, Mulligan began to build a team. The first step was to identify some early supporters who were willing to guide the campaign and make initial introductions. She needed people who would put in the work and help fundraise, recruit volunteers, and keep track of all the loose ends. Often when a candidate announces, she is assured by hordes of people around them that she can count on their support. Yet when the time comes to call in those favors, finding people who are *actually* willing to put in the work can prove much more difficult.

The 55th District was made up mainly of the two suburban cities of Des Plaines and Park Ridge. It was clear Mulligan, as a resident of Des Plaines, needed to make inroads in Park Ridge, where she was raised as a child. As the more Republican of the two cities, there were more votes to be had in Park Ridge. Not to mention, she wanted to take on Pullen on her own turf.

When news of Mulligan's announcement spread to other news outlets, it was no surprise that coverage focused on her being prochoice, Catholic, and a Republican. "If I get in front of enough groups, talk to enough people, and shake enough hands, [Pullen will] be really sorry she didn't campaign," Mulligan confidently proclaimed to one newspaper.[3] That opening line of her campaign was perhaps prescient; Pullen would give her and the challenge little attention. Naïveté was a word some would use to describe her confidence in believing at that point she could take out a fourteen-year incumbent. Pullen had experienced impassioned election challenges before, but Mulligan felt Pullen was especially odious. It wasn't just her politics, but the way she treated people and went about spreading her message. Mulligan found her to be arrogant and dismissive.

Most of Pullen's previous challengers were Democrats who, because of the makeup of the district, stood little chance at ousting her. Mulligan knew she would be labeled as a liberal for some of her left-leaning proclivities on social issues, so she tried to highlight her Republican bona fides right out of the gate. "I'm not some Johnny-come-lately Republican," she told a paper covering the announcement.[4] She talked about her family's Republican leanings, her past involvement in GOP politics, and why her brand of politics was more representative of the district. Mulligan's case to voters would be that Pullen was simply too extreme. It would be a difficult needle to thread in a partisan primary where candidates are typically rewarded by voters the further to the right they move. In a primary, candidates have every incentive to take extreme positions, pander to disparate special interest groups, and deliver lofty campaign promises that will be all but impossible to keep once elected. It's all about telling voters what they want to hear. Mulligan, on the other hand, would be asking primary voters to reward her for her self-perceived moderation.

Mary Ann Irvine was sitting in her living room reading the *Park Ridge Herald* when she read on the front page that a prochoice, Republican, Catholic was launching a campaign to unseat Penny Pullen. "Oh c'mon. This can't be true," she said to her husband in disbelief as she read the headline.[5] A communications professional at a trade association in Chicago, Irvine was intrigued. At fifty-one, Irvine had short, sandy blonde curls and a thin frame. She spoke in a manner that made others feel she had common sense, a tone that was calm but confident, almost motherly. Irvine had paid close attention to political battles like those over the ERA and early abortion rulings. She was the kind of feminist who lived in the suburbs, worked, and raised a family, the type of person who didn't fit the caricature painted by many on the right of those who ascribed to her political views. Over the years, she had volunteered her time to other challengers to Pullen, but having a legitimate Republican launch a campaign was different. Having been involved locally as the president of the League of Women Voters and eventually a member of the Park Ridge City Council for two terms, Irvine had a lot to offer the newcomer. Politically, she felt Pullen was too conservative for the district.

Mulligan and Mary Ann Irvine had never met, so Irvine looked up the now-announced candidate's name in the phone book and dialed her right then and there in her living room. Irvine needed very little convincing to help, and she was willing to do whatever it took to make a change. When the phone went to an answering machine, she left an eager message. "I'm an alderman in Park Ridge. I see you're running against Pullen. Thank you so much for doing that. I can get you many people to pass your petitions," she excitedly recounted to the machine.[6] There had been an overwhelming response to Mulligan's announcement, and the early excitement underscored even more why she needed help keeping things together. After a busy week, Mulligan finally returned the call. When the two women ultimately connected, Irvine spared no time helping gather signatures to get Mulligan's name on the ballot.

The first test of any candidate is gaining access to the ballot. If this initial hurdle can't be overcome, the campaign ends. Candidates can run as write-ins, but the logistical difficulties of mounting a serious write-in challenge are almost always prohibitive. Some states make it difficult for newcomers to throw their hats in the ring in an effort to protect the old guard. In presidential primaries, the party plays a particularly important role in dictating these rules, with some state parties simply demanding candidates write a check as high as $20,000 to get their name on the ballot. Ballot access is democracy at its dumbest.

Illinois had a relatively low threshold, requiring primary election candidates to submit just 500 signatures from registered Republican voters in the district. While the minimum number was a modest 500, candidates generally need to gather extra to be safe from a legal challenge. Once filed, candidates risk being thrown off the ballot if the legitimacy of their signatures are disputed by an opponent, an activist, or even a random member of the public. Incumbent candidates who have experience navigating the labyrinthine election system are particularly apt at launching signature challenges, further wielding the tremendous power of incumbency. Not just any person can sign a petition, and there are a multitude of reasons why a signature might be disqualified: the signer is not a registered voter, doesn't live in the district, isn't a member of the candidate's political party, or if they've already signed another petition. Mulligan was taking no chances on that front.

As time went on, Mulligan decided to name Irvine as her campaign chair. Having a public face in the community would be a boon to the operation, and Mary Ann Irvine knew where to find the right people. Mulligan held one of the first campaign events in Irvine's living room, right where she first learned about Mulligan's bid.

Mulligan soon after chose a woman named Diddy Blythe as cochair. Originally from the Philadelphia area, forty-eight-year-old Blythe had the gift of gab. She could speak to almost anyone about anything with her soothing, syrupy voice that made you want to listen, almost southern but without the twang. She knew how to read people and could sniff out baloney. Having worked as a lobbyist for the Junior League of Illinois, she understood the inner workings of Springfield and the politics of the 55th District. What did people want? Who was on the up-and-up? Who was sleeping with whom? Diddy Blythe was the kind of person who knew everyone's needs and never missed a birthday. These things weren't gossip; they were business.

Diddy Blythe had been approached about running against Pullen originally, but decided against it. She was a single working parent with a thirteen-year-old at home, and living a double life in Springfield was not in the cards. But like Mary Ann Irvine, she felt Pullen's politics didn't represent the district. Pullen simply voted no on too many pieces of legislation, a pattern she found frustrating. In lieu of running herself, supporting Mulligan was the best way to volunteer her time.

The first encounter, as with Irvine, was a simple phone call. Mulligan dialed up Diddy Blythe out of the blue and asked her if she'd be willing to help the campaign. For any candidate, a certain level of audacity is required with being comfortable asking strangers to help for almost nothing in return. Blythe was hesitant at first given how new to the scene Mulligan was. "I don't know who you are, but why don't we go out for breakfast?" she asked.[7] So they did. Mulligan suggested they meet outside of Park Ridge at the Walker Brothers Pancake House in Wilmette, a classic breakfast spot about twenty-five minutes from town. Blythe thought meeting out of town was strange at first, but she chalked it up to Mulligan wanting to keep things quiet as she kicked the campaign into high gear. She was more concerned with whether someone so green had the wherewithal to mount a proper campaign against Pullen.

As the women sat down for breakfast and sipped coffee, what began as a simple chat blossomed into a two-hour conversation. Blythe could feel Mulligan's sincere passion when she spoke. She radiated confidence and made it clear she wasn't kidding around. Blythe found her charming, and quickly agreed to help out. *Rosemary didn't know anyone*, she thought, but she could help fill that gap and start making connections for her across the district.

Others in the community quickly came out forward to offer support for Mulligan. People would pledge their time and promise to make contributions to the campaign. They would tell her to put yard signs in their lawn, something she hadn't yet thought about nor did she know where to begin to get them printed. She would have to take things one step at a time and trust that things would come together. It was November 1989 and Mulligan was making connections fast, but she still lacked someone with proper campaign chops. Simply put, nobody in her growing circle knew how to run a *real* political operation.

Mulligan had recently learned about a prochoice political action committee called Personal PAC that formed and opened an office in the Chicago Loop. Their mission was to give prochoice candidates a boost in their races and try to turn the tide in Springfield on abortion. For years, abortion had been a somewhat bipartisan issue, and even the Democratic speaker of the House had proclaimed his prolife views and permitted legislation to move forward on the issue despite opposition inside his caucus. For many Chicago Democrats, the influence of the archdiocese in Chicago meant that abortion remained an issue on which they continued to defy the party platform. Personal PAC aimed to show candidates they could win with a different stance. And the *Webster* decision became the perfect recruiting tool for volunteers and donors. The Supreme Court's ruling generated a renewed sense of urgency among a group of voters that was politically apathetic and unmotivated just months earlier. About a month after Personal PAC's office opening, Mulligan called up the headquarters in November of 1989 and asked for a meeting. She was on a mission, and she had already proven she wasn't above asking strangers for help.

Terry Cosgrove had recently been hired as the first executive director of Personal PAC. Tall and lanky, Cosgrove had short black hair just a cut above a buzz. He was painfully familiar with Pullen for her abortion legislation, controversial AIDS initiatives, and opposition to the Equal Rights Amendment. Just weeks earlier the organization was operating at their founder's kitchen table in suburban Winnetka, and Cosgrove knew Personal PAC needed a marquee race for the 1990 election to help put it on the map. But Cosgrove was a shrewd operator and understood it would be a challenge to take out a fourteen-year incumbent, as enticing as the prospect was. Pullen, after all, was in House Republican leadership and had a statewide—if not national—following. Still, he decided it was worth the time to meet with Mulligan and allow her to make her case.

Mulligan met with Terry Cosgrove and Personal PAC's main funder Marcie Love at the Pickwick Restaurant, the spot where she had first been convinced to run following the rally in Park Ridge. When the three sat down for lunch, Mulligan was enthusiastic. She talked about her previous political involvement and what drove her to run. She knew it would be a challenge to defeat Pullen, but if anyone was going to do it, it would be her. Considering they had never heard of Mulligan, Cosgrove and Marcie Love were skeptical. But Mulligan's sincere energy caught their attention. She was intelligent and informed about the issues. Not to mention, she had a good sense of humor.

Leaving the restaurant, Cosgrove regrouped with Love. "She's really serious, isn't she?" he said. Winning this race would be a huge success for

Personal PAC. There were tons of other campaigns they could focus on, though, and they agreed it might be worth investing some time in other candidates. But a few days later, Cosgrove was sorting through his mail when a large manilla envelope from Rosemary Mulligan appeared. When he opened it up, a stack of fifty business cards fell out on his desk and a handwritten note. "I really appreciate your help!" Mulligan wrote.[8] The message to Cosgrove was clear: I'm not asking for your help, I'm telling you to get on board. For Terry Cosgrove, that was enough.

Having grown up nearby, Cosgrove was well aware of the 55th District's ruby red political leanings. He knew the campaign for Mulligan would require a well-oiled operation, and he decided the ultimate goal would be identifying 10,000 prochoice voters in the district they could turn out in a Republican primary just four months later. With little more than a hunch, he felt there were enough Republican voters in the district who disagreed with Pullen's rigid stance on abortion and just needed a reason to be driven to the polls.

As recently as the 1990s, party identification was not a clear sign of a politician's view on abortion; prolife Democrats existed throughout the country as well as prochoice Republicans. Today, stances on the issue mostly fall along party lines. Today, there are only a handful of prochoice Republicans and prolife Democrats Congress in Washington. Voters, however, are actually much more divided on the issue than the positions of the people representing them would portend. In 2020, three out of every ten Democrats—as well as Republicans—disagreed with their party's official stance on abortion.[9]

Terry Cosgrove was no stranger to confrontation. When he was a student at University of Illinois Urbana-Champaign in 1980, he was kicked out of a bar for dancing with his boyfriend. The bouncer tapped him on the shoulder and informed him there were plenty of girls to dance with. When Cosgrove didn't get the hint, the bouncer asked him again to stop dancing. Eventually, the owners of the bar asked him to leave. Cosgrove refused, and the police were called.

A public accommodation ordinance in the city had recently outlawed discrimination on the basis of sexual orientation, but the bar owners either didn't realize the effect of the ordinance or didn't care. When law enforcement arrived, Cosgrove had the officers sign a statement saying the only reason he and his boyfriend were asked to leave was because they were two men dancing. The next day, he went to Champaign City Hall before a city commission to report the situation and eventually sued with the help of a LGBT civil rights organization called Lambda Legal. The case resulted in one of the first settlements of its kind involving violation of a nondiscrimination ordinance.[10]

Cosgrove had been involved in college as a campus leader in various liberal causes. He was a student of politics and soon learned the ropes working around political campaigns. When he was asked to run Personal PAC, he was delighted. Of all the issues, reproductive rights was the one that motivated him the most. Terry felt it was not the government's business to involve itself in a woman's intimate medical decisions.

He began to draft plans for the race against Pullen and work closely with Mulligan on next steps. Creating a campaign plan involves working backward from Election Day, so Cosgrove started with the number of votes needed to win, a plan for how to raise money and recruit volunteers, and a countdown of the days until the polls open. Cosgrove found a campaign manager for Mulligan and helped recruit other young staffers. The staffers he brought in would be working the office and out in the field running the day-to-day minutiae of the campaign. They would keep a steady stream of volunteers coming in, plan events in the area, and knock on doors across the district. Behind it all, Terry Cosgrove would be pulling the strings.

Still, the first step was getting Mulligan's name on the ballot. Unlike her opponent, Mulligan didn't have a built-in volunteer base that could spring into action at a moment's notice. Her volunteers went door to door, stood outside shopping centers, and eventually garnered the 500 valid signatures required. Many of the volunteers came from outside the district, driven mostly toward the campaign because of their deep dislike of Penny Pullen. Within just a few weeks, the campaign was prepared to meet the December 15 deadline and had enough signatures to avoid a challenge from a potentially litigious opponent. Thanks to their quick work, Mulligan's name would be on the March 20, 1990, Republican primary ballot just a few months later.

Illinois law specified that candidates were listed in the order in which they filed. If they filed at the same time, there would be a lottery. In a close race where every vote counts, having your name first on the ballot can make the difference between packing your bags for Springfield and retreating home with your tail between your legs. Some voters, no matter how much noise a campaign makes, will just choose the first name they see on the ballot. Much to the Mulligan volunteers' chagrin, Pullen's team beat them to the punch. Still, it was relief that step one of the campaign was complete.

With Mulligan's name officially on the ballot, the next assignment to tackle was fundraising. There's an old adage about the "three Ms" of politics—message, momentum, money. But for most campaigns, especially those down ballot, the "three Ms" are slightly different—money, money,

money. The smaller the race, the less important media coverage is for a candidate. Instead of news coverage, local races have to rely on their own means—mailers, phone calls, and door-to-door canvassers—to get their message out to voters.

Raising money was new challenge for Mulligan. When a candidate first announces, the biggest rush is typically to post strong first-quarter numbers. The numbers are a show of strength not only to the media, but to the other campaign. Throughout January and February of 1990, Mulligan held fundraisers in living rooms and dining halls. She met with everyone and anyone who would sit down with her. When they threw together an event, supporters pitched in and made food at home in lieu of expensive catering. It was a grassroots effort, to be sure. Diddy Blythe spent a lot of her time calling people asking them to come to fundraisers and became somewhat of a social chair for the campaign. People gave what they could initially, many skeptical of just how far Mulligan would make it.

PACs are often an easy source of money for campaigns. Candidates fill out a questionnaire, say a few hellos, and get a maxed-out contribution without lifting so much as a finger. But as a challenger to a longtime incumbent, Mulligan didn't have that luxury and most groups decided to back Pullen by default. Pullen had a record to run on that they could measure against their interests, while supporting a newcomer would be a risk. Aided by the power of incumbency, Pullen had amassed a huge lead in fundraising. Pullen's national involvement in the Republican party also helped her make inroads with larger contributors outside the district. She had served as a GOP committeewoman in Illinois from 1984 to 1988 after defeating an incumbent committeewoman named Crete Harvey in a bitter party infight. Pullen served in the position for one term, but it allowed her unrestricted access to donors and high-ranking party officials. Whenever President Reagan or Vice President Bush came to Illinois for fundraisers or campaign events, she would be seated just a few feet away at the dais.

To make up for her fundraising deficit, state and national prochoice groups began pouring money into Mulligan's campaign. "Did we go looking for her? No. Are we tickled? Yes," said the leader of the National Abortion Rights Action League in Illinois when asked about Mulligan's campaign.[11] "When people heard there was a viable candidate [opposing Pullen] we about held a party," said another prochoice leader.[12]

Many candidates are encouraged to run because they're approached by a political insider who pledges to bolster them from behind the scenes. But Mulligan hadn't been recruited by any group with the implicit promise to support her candidacy. No VIP or party official courted her, nor did she ask for anyone's permission. Mulligan made the decision to run because she felt she was the right candidate. Everything else, in her view, would fall into place.

But even with national groups pouring in resources, Mulligan still needed local money to compete. Terry Cosgrove and others had to force Mulligan to spend time on the phone calling through lists of donors and making her pitch. Each call meant pleading for an investment in the campaign.

The truth is, Mulligan hated asking people for money and wasn't very good at it. The more time she spent on the phone begging for money, the less time she had interacting with voters and understanding their concerns. There are some rare candidates who get a rush from fundraising and view it as a challenge. Rosemary Mulligan was not one of them.

While Diddy Blythe helped bring people along to fundraisers, Mary Ann Irvine concentrated on the volunteer operation with less than three months to go until the March 1990 primary. She hadn't been as intensely involved in previous campaigns in the 55th District, but she felt this campaign would be worth the extra effort. Raising a family and working full time made the time commitments challenging, so after she came home from working downtown Chicago in the evening, she would spend the rest of her night working with the campaign. She called volunteers to schedule them to knock on doors the next weekend or phone bank. She called volunteers to have them lick envelopes and help with mailers. She called volunteers to help staff events and fill in for odd jobs. Pretty soon, Mulligan became the first person Mary Ann Irvine spoke to in the morning and the last person at night.

In many ways, the time spent working together with people during an election can seem like it's longer than it is, and the unique bonding experience makes for quick friendships for people working together down in the trenches. Irvine experienced this firsthand, as did dozens of other people who felt a calling to work for Rosemary Mulligan.

As the election drew closer, it was time to open a campaign office in the district that would serve as a gathering place for volunteers. No more kitchen tables and living room meetings. A space was secured in Uptown Park Ridge just a short walk away from city hall where Mulligan had spoken at the prochoice rally just a few months back. Located on the quaintly named Main Street, the space was just steps from the Metra commuter train, so those commuting from Chicago to work on the campaign had easy access. It was a central location in the 55th District, right in the heart of town. Not to mention, it was just a block away from Penny Pullen's government office. Putting a stake in the ground just a few paces away would let Pullen know the team was serious.

The quintessential campaign office, it was a crummy, unfinished room that left much to the imagination. Located on the second floor of a two-story office building, it overlooked the train tracks nearby. The campaign decided on a Saturday opening that they would use to draw attention to the race and recruit new volunteers. "Begin Again with Mulligan," proclaimed the banners displayed for the local reporters in attendance.[13] A smart staff never loses out on an opportunity to push out the campaign's message, and this team made sure no occasion was squandered.

As the campaign progressed, Diddy Blythe took on the role of body woman to the candidate. A body person accompanies the candidate at all times and makes sure nothing falls through the cracks, from collecting business cards while the candidate is making her way through a crowd to carrying her bags. She drove Mulligan to events, briefed her before she walked in the door, and kept her on a strict schedule. But Mulligan never quite got used to the grind. With the candidate still constantly running late, Blythe's main job became getting Mulligan on time to her events. In many cases, that meant going to her house and dragging her out while she was still getting ready.

Mulligan always made sure to put her hair up, sport the right shoes, and wrap a carefully coordinated scarf around her neck for most occasions—red, white, and blue at veterans' halls or an ode to the flag of the local ethnic group (white and red for Polish, green for Irish). Mulligan understood that elections are popularity contests, after all, and nobody wants a shlub representing them.

Campaigning doesn't come naturally to everyone, and Mulligan was no exception. At events, Blythe would push her to work the crowd. "No, you're not done," she'd say. "There's half a room. Go on!"[14] But once Mulligan got the hang of things, she became a skilled retail politician. She wanted to truly understand the needs of the people she spoke with. What were they thinking? Why did they think that way? How could she help? She became comfortable with crowds and meeting new people who had things to ask of her.

For every state legislative campaign, there are obligatory stops that must be made around town, from the local VFW hall and Rotary Club to the chamber of commerce and real estate boards. Each faction is civically engaged and has its own needs and wants. Their members vote. So it's important for the local candidate to show face and, at the very least, make them feel heard.

Gathered at the Des Plaines Elks Lodge for a meeting of the local Kiwanis chapter, Mulligan hurriedly scarfed down a plate of Salisbury steak and headed to the front of the room to face the mostly male crowd. Before the roughly thirty-five gray-haired members listened to Mulligan's stump speech, they led one another in the Pledge of Allegiance and a baritone version of "My Country Tis of Thee." With the formalities finished, Mulligan appeared at the podium while the audience clapped to welcome her. She quickly pounced on her opponent. "If you will think about it, I think you have not seen our incumbent in this area for a while," she asserted, pointing out Pullen's seeming absence from events like these. "I think that's sad."[15] The woman who at first stuck strictly to notes quickly became adept at giving off-the-cuff remarks to almost any audience, and she wasn't afraid to throw a punch in the process.

The 55th was Penny Pullen country, and Pullen made sure the Mulligan campaign knew it. As soon as Mulligan announced her intention to run late the year before, yard signs began to pop up around the district. Pullen and her supporters were used to the drill. Each year, they would stake out the most visible spots for signs at corners on busy streets and crowded intersections. Businesses that attracted lots of street traffic were particularly helpful. For years, Pullen had cultivated these cherished relationships and had only to say the word to put a sign up each election. The signs posted across the district mean little to nothing about the actual outcome, but candidates themselves obsess over seeing their name in lawns and at businesses around town. When yards become littered with these not-so-subtle endorsements, it creates a perception in the candidate's mind of momentum. Legions of campaign staffers have explained to their candidate for decades that indeed, signs don't vote. But the ritual continues anyway, and Mulligan had a great deal of ground to make up.

Her catching up wasn't just limited to finding strategic places for signs, but getting more visibility in the press. One of the easiest ways for a candidate to make up ground in this area is to challenge their opponent to a debate. But Pullen had no incentive to appear on a stage with Mulligan. Most local campaigns or state legislative races held these sorts of events with groups such as the League of Women Voters, but the League hadn't been too friendly to Pullen in the past, so she had even less reason to show up.

Eventually, Mulligan's campaign decided that in lieu of a formal debate, a debate about debates would be more appropriate. The goal would be to make Pullen look petty by not agreeing to appear with her. Mulligan started by challenging Pullen in a formal letter to a series of five debates. She suggested innocuous, local topics like property tax relief, the area's flood problem, and education. "The voters have a right to hear what their state representative has done and intends to do for the district," Mulligan insisted.

Pullen's campaign responded in kind. "Thank you for the offer to assist me in communicating my views and record to the voters of the 55th Representative District," she wrote in reply. "I have an extensive program planned to accomplish this goal, and it does not include engaging you in debate."[16] In other words, thanks but no thanks.

Pullen's strategy was a familiar one. Conventional wisdom says the candidate running ahead is better off not appearing on a debate stage with a volatile opponent. Why risk it? Pullen had won her last race by a 2–1 margin and the last time she faced a serious challenge was nearly a decade before. "It looks like I got about 35 percent of the vote, which isn't bad considering what the district is," one of Pullen's previous opponents once observed after her resounding defeat, underscoring the difficulties of mounting a serious challenge.[17] Term after term, voters in the district had sent Pullen back to Springfield with an overwhelming mandate to continue her work. A letter to the editor in the paper echoed this view. "What's to debate?" a voter asked rhetorically. "Rosemary is a Democrat at heart masquerading as a Republican," he asserted.[18]

The campaign continued to hire staff and recruit new volunteers who would dedicate their free time to the effort. One of Mulligan's volunteer coordinators had previously worked on the campaign of Lucy Killea, a California Democrat who ran successfully for state legislature. Killea became nationally known as the first elected official in the United States to be publicly denied Holy Communion by her local Catholic church for her pro-choice views. Today, Killea counts among her peers Joe Biden, Nancy Pelosi, and John Kerry as Catholic Democrats who have been denied communion because of their views on abortion.[19]

Mulligan had her own run-in with her local Catholic church. When she and her son Matt went to attend mass one Sunday, they grabbed the church bulletin on the way in and started chatting with the priest who was greeting parishioners as they entered the pews. When the priest noticed Mulligan and her son wearing campaign buttons, he paused. He insisted they take the buttons off or leave. It finally hit Mulligan that she was no longer just a regular citizen, and people around town were beginning to know who she was. While they were shocked at the priest's ask, it likely had more to do with the fact that they had surreptitiously placed flyers on all the parishioners' windshields the previous Sunday. Still, the incident left her with a bad taste in her mouth.

By February of 1990, Mulligan felt the campaign's positive momentum building. She had had confidence since the beginning, but things were beginning to progress. She had a core of volunteers. She was raising money.

And the campaign was getting great news coverage. But unbeknownst to her, Terry Cosgrove and Personal PAC had commissioned a poll on the race. The result was clear. With just six weeks to go until the March 20 primary, Pullen had a commanding 53 percent of Republican voters, while Mulligan was garnering just 22 percent. Twenty-five percent were undecided. "What are we going to do?" a campaign staffer asked Terry Cosgrove. "We're going to pretend we never took this poll and we're not going to tell Rosemary," he said.[20] It wasn't worth breaking her spirit.

Penny Pullen making a phone call in her Park Ridge campaign office in 1990.
Photo Credit: *Daily Herald*

7

Raccoons, Reporters, and Rapists' Rights

You'll have no problem if you will just keep your legs crossed.

The political sphere has sometimes been referred to as "ugly Hollywood"—in both senses of the word. In Washington and state capitals across the country, celebrity and status often trump substance. In ugly Hollywood, there have always been politicians who yearn for heads to turn when they enter the room and live for the faint whispers of "That's Representative *So-and-So*" as they pass by. Like the siren's song, the allure of the microphone is irresistible, whether when grandstanding during a committee hearing or schmoozing with reporters between meetings. When running for office, these wannabe celebrities—the kind that actually make decisions that affect us all—dream of voters clapping enthusiastically at their every brilliant word rather than having to answer angry mobs of constituents at a community town hall. Some politicians just want to be loved.

For Penny Pullen, commanding respect was more important than being loved. The legislature was a place for important business, not a social club. Still, she made fast friends with many of her fellow legislators, especially those with whom she shared an ideological bond. For many years, Pullen's desk on the floor of the Illinois House was next to Ralph Barger, a conservative Republican representing the upper-middle-class suburb of Wheaton, roughly an hour west of Chicago.

The former mayor was now in his late sixties and sported a thick mustache with a dense head of hair. During World War II, Barger had served in the Army Air Corps in Europe and later opened his own printing company. Like Pullen's path to politics, his also involved a death that created an opening.[1] After losing the GOP primary for state representative in 1982 by just 77 votes, his opponent died of an aneurysm.[2] Barger was appointed by the local Republican party to take his place and had served in the legislature ever since. Pullen viewed him as an uncle-like figure who teased her frequently on the state House floor, and the two maintained a friendly rapport. Barger didn't speak much on the record in the House chamber, but his warm presence was felt nonetheless.

Like his friend Penny Pullen, Ralph Barger was facing a tough primary challenge in 1990. Seated in his office with a group of five women from the local chapter of the American Association of University Women the previous November, Barger put his foot in his mouth. "You'll have no problem if you will just keep your legs crossed," the sexagenarian told the young women after they expressed concerns about his views on abortion.[3] Needless to say, Barger's vulgar quip did not sit well with many women in his district, and Pullen was enlisted to help clean up the mess. For a man who typically was quite careful with his words, this blunder was now endangering his career and sparking raucous opposition in the district.

"We need Ralph in Springfield," Pullen wrote in a letter to voters in his district sent a few weeks before the March 1990 primary. Her name lent Barger credibility from a high-ranking Republican woman. "We need his quiet wisdom, his determination to hold down taxes and spending and to provide job opportunities through free enterprise, and yes, we need his humor, painful as it is at times."[4]

As with Barger after his controversial remarks, wary eyes were on Pullen's race as well. After she introduced her *Webster* look-alike bill in Springfield, the local chapter of the National Organization for Women awarded Pullen—in absentia—their annual "Turkey" award for "being a disaster for women."[5] But left-leaning groups like NOW had always been a thorn in Pullen's side, so their tongue-in-cheek attacks did little to move her.

Aside from her legislation designed to restrict abortion, Pullen kept her head down both in Springfield and back in the 55th District. She immersed herself in the quintessential issues that are the bulk of any state legislator's day-to-day activities. Her office flooded taxpayers' mailboxes with instructions about how to appeal their property tax assessments, she held a health fair for senior citizens, and when she could, she continued helping out with some of her colleagues' political races. Serving in the legislature was technically a part-time job and many legislators had other jobs, but not Pullen. She was all in, committed to serving her constituents.

Filing her nominating petitions to get on the ballot came easy. After fourteen years in the House, Pullen had a loyal supporter base that could kick into action at a moment's notice. She brought her stack of petitions to the State Board of Elections along with a coterie of volunteers and photographers in December of 1989. With a quick turnaround between a January swearing-in for winning candidates and a December deadline for filing petitions to run again just eleven months later, her campaign remained in constant contact with volunteers through newsletters about her legislative activities and the progress of her primary race and upcoming general election. These volunteers were an invaluable resource to the campaign, and the team referred to them as their "Penny Pals."

Finding people to work on a political campaign can be difficult. Getting them to return—whether the next election cycle or the next day—can be even more challenging. When a candidate runs for governor or president, there is an implicit understanding that time on the trail could result in a state or federal job. But on state legislative races and even campaigns for Congress, there is little for a self-interested person to gain from helping out.

For smaller races, the job description for a volunteer coordinator may as well list "begging" as a required skill, because sometimes it's the only tool available. Aside from that appeal, there are generally four emotions believed to motivate voters and volunteers—hope, fear, pride, and anger. If you don't have at least one of these that registers with volunteers, good luck filling the phone banks and licking enough envelopes at the campaign office. Fortunately for both Pullen and her challenger, there was no shortage of hope, fear, pride—and most importantly—anger in the 55th District.

When the time came for endorsements, the process for Pullen was just as perfunctory as the signature gathering. The most coveted endorsement in a Republican primary was that of the local Republican organization, the Maine Township GOP. When Pullen first ran in 1976 for the seat to replace her old boss, Representative Robert Juckett, she campaigned hard for the support of all the local precinct captains whose votes were necessary for the endorsement. Since then, she had carefully cultivated and maintained relationships with all the local leaders. In short order, the Maine Township GOP unanimously endorsed her for another term. It was a sign that, within the party at least, there wasn't much appetite for a challenge. Penny Pullen was their candidate.

Aside from the Maine Township GOP, one of the most important party groups in the area was the Republican Women of Park Ridge. In Republican politics, women's groups are an important and powerful constituency that hold sway over the party. The 55th District was no exception. The group hosted a "Men's Night" event for all the local candidates to come and talk to its members and their spouses. While the attendees sipped wine and ate assorted cheeses, those running for mayor, city council, and other offices made their respective cases to the group with a few minutes set aside for each candidate. It was the first time Pullen and Mulligan would appear together—and it would be one of their last. After speaking to her accomplishments over the course of her several terms and what she hoped to achieve in the next, Pullen thanked Mulligan for jumping into the race. It was a shot across the bow, cockily and condescendingly acknowledging the slim chances of the challenger in the audience.

Big names came out to support Pullen too, something Mulligan simply didn't have. Ed and Virginia McCaskey, owners of the Chicago Bears, hosted a brunch in Pullen's honor to help launch her bid for an eighth term. The McCaskeys were not just constituents, but also big fans of her prolife advocacy. Richard DeVos, the CEO of Amway and a well-known Republican donor, came in from Michigan to hold a fundraiser. A Republican luminary, his family would carry on the legacy when his daughter-in-law Betsy would serve as Donald Trump's secretary of education. Richard DeVos had worked with Pullen on the AIDS commission, and they had gotten to know one another at various national party functions. There were dozens of important races for the House, Senate, and governors' mansions to which DeVos could contribute his time and money that year. DeVos, one of the richest men in the world and a key leader in the national GOP, chose to spend some of his fortune in Illinois's tiny 55th state legislative district. If there was one thing Pullen had, it was a Rolodex that other state candidates could only envy.

• • •

Running for office is a full-time job. And then some. What many who have never been around a campaign don't understand is that even local races are all-consuming. When the sun is up, you have to dial for dollars during business hours and knock on doors. When night comes, the candidate plans for the days ahead—prepping for events, studying up for speeches and candidate forums, answering mail and writing thank-you notes. On top of this, a candidate has a personal life to deal with. And if you don't have an accommodating employer, spouse or partner, or enough cash saved up to get you through the race, it becomes nearly impossible to make it all work. Candidates, with very few exceptions, are not permitted to pay themselves and the expenses their funds can cover are very limited. For many, this is a total barrier to entry, and Rosemary Mulligan felt fortunate to have such a strong base of support around her.

Mulligan maintained a grueling schedule while still working full time as a paralegal. Her law firm was accommodating, even supportive of her bid, and the firm allowed Mulligan to take time off when necessary. She agreed to take a leave of absence as the primary drew closer. With just a few weeks to go before the March 20 primary, Mulligan was now dedicating 100 percent of her time toward the campaign. And as it looked doubtful that she would have a chance to debate her rival, Mulligan took the time to speak with anyone and everyone who would host her individually.

Campaign staffers continued chauffeuring Mulligan to her events and attempting to keep her on time. But her chronic lateness was proving problematic with so many appearances stacked up and Election Day drawing closer. In a tight race where every vote would count, Mulligan's campaign didn't want to give supporters a reason to second guess their choice. So the team devised a plan to fix Mulligan's tardiness by lying to her about the start times of events. When an event began at noon, they'd tell her to be ready at 11 a.m. and they'd stroll in just on time. Problem solved.

To someone hearing her for the first time, Mulligan could seem almost nervous. She spoke with a subtle Chicago accent, stressing her vowels ever so slightly. Her voice usually sounded like it was on the cusp of cracking. If she was talking on the radio, her speech might not come off as convincing. But in person, Mulligan was always well-prepared and warm. When she spoke, she was confident and had strong answers to questions. She had done her homework and studied up on the issues that were actually facing the legislature, not just empty talking points. At the same time, she never shied away from playing the role of attack dog.

"It's an embarrassment, and I'll say that straight out," she told a crowd at a local Jaycees chapter during their March meeting, attempting to paint her opponent as out of touch.[6] Mulligan's appearance often served to soften the blow of her sharp rhetoric. She dressed professionally, usually in a neatly pressed skirt suit or a blouse with a solid-colored jacket and matching scarf tied neatly around her neck. Her lapel was never empty. She complemented her outfits with oversized flowers—cherry-red chrysanthemums, bleach white carnations adorned with a subtle touch of baby's breath—or a dark blue campaign pin decorated with an elephant to showcase her party loyalty. Pointing to specific votes, Mulligan made the case that Pullen was an extremist. Pullen had voted against compensating local law enforcement officers hurt in the line of duty; she opposed funding for social services; and she had sponsored the odious bill that Mulligan labeled a "Rapists' Bill of Rights"—the one that would allow the father of an unborn child to have a say before a woman had an abortion. When the speeches were finished, Mulligan would work the room by shaking hands and trying to meet as many people as possible. She was quickly becoming a comfortable, easy-going campaigner. In private, she was even more confident. "I'm gonna beat that bitch," she'd sometimes tell close supporters and staff.[7]

Mulligan's staff continued to keep things humming while Mulligan was out on the trail. Both campaigns had an unprecedented number of supporters willing to put in time. Sometimes volunteers come to a campaign with naïve preconceptions of what they'll be tasked with doing. The job is usually simple: sit at a white card table in a hollowed-out office or an unfurnished room or an empty strip mall storefront and call as many voters as possible. If you're lucky, you might get to knock on some doors. And if you're really lucky, you might be able to help with some mundane office work or attend events with the candidate.

Campaign offices are a personal injury lawyer's dream. Within a few weeks of opening, cardboard boxes stacked to the ceiling fill nearly every square foot of empty space. One by one, volunteers assemble yard signs by sticking two-pronged metal stakes into the mini billboards made of corrugated plastic. The most dedicated sign builders come away with steel-stained hands, a badge of honor for their hard work.

When the time comes to construct phone banks, young campaign staffers thread wires throughout the office like needleworkers embroidering their next creation. Across the carpeted floor, phone lines are hastily secured with duct tape to prevent the cords from spreading like a wild kudzu vine throughout the office. Cheap metal chairs are tightly packed around folding tables. Office supplies beget office supplies.

Inside smaller boxes scattered about sit thousands of pieces of literature yet to be showered across the district—flyers, door hangers, and palm cards. In a mad dash before a shift, volunteers grab their goods and pack it into the trunk of their car in the hopes their haul will last. Even for volunteers, the campaign seeps into their everyday life with literature scattered on the floors of their cars or across the dashboard for all to see.

As phone banks fill, the office kitchen counters are crammed with snacks to keep people satiated and dialing. A pot of hot coffee is always brewing in the background. Pizza is ordered with the dependable consistency of a nightly call to prayer. Candy is carefully laid out in bowls for volunteers to suck on between calls. Just as an exhausted parent gives anything to calm their crying child, campaign staff provides volunteers whatever they need to keep on working.

On each table, paper scripts guide each caller step-by-step through the drill. The mission is simple: gather data for the campaign. Does that person support us? Oppose us? Are they undecided? Reaching that point, however, is more of an art. It requires a conversation. And a conversation that usually begins by interrupting a person's day.

Dialers are carefully instructed to introduce themselves and ask if the person intends to vote in the Republican primary in March. Then comes the inquisition. *What issues are most important to you?* A response, followed by a carefully crafted pitch. *Did you know that Rosemary Mulligan supports . . . ?* Phone banking is no different from when a salesperson calls you to pitch a product, except the product is the candidate on your ballot.

Mulligan loved seeing her volunteers around the office. Whenever she showed up, her arms were filled with cookies, candy, chips and dip, donuts, and whatever else she could feed to the masses. She felt an immense sense of gratitude toward those who had given their free time to help her, especially many strangers who she'd only recently met. Mulligan quickly learned the power of a handwritten note, too.

Next to fundraising and attending events, one of the most essential jobs of a local candidate is much simpler: knocking on doors. Most legislative districts are quite small. In Illinois, the average district has fewer than 100,000 citizens. Because of this, some of the best use of the candidate's time is simply meeting those you're trying to convince. No mail, no TV, no surrogates. Just face-to-face contact. Some people think a candidate just goes door to door at random to get their message out. But in reality, campaigns have to maximize their time by targeting their activities. In the early days of the campaign, that typically means aiming for the ever-elusive persuadable voter who can be convinced to come to your side. As time draws nearer to Election Day, campaigns focus on turning out their already identified supporters and reliably partisan voters. In a primary where two candidates are competing for the same pot of people, this calculation becomes even more important.

Mulligan relied principally on the lists that Terry Cosgrove, the head of Personal PAC, provided the campaign. In the cold days of February and March, she canvassed the district as heavily as she could, even if it meant trekking out in the snow and slush. Cosgrove and the team had planned to focus on prochoice primary voters. But many voters didn't care about the hot-button topic of abortion, so Mulligan tried to emphasize what she would do for her future constituents on other kitchen-table issues. Taxes. Area flooding. Corruption in Illinois. Still, abortion was front and center. When she walked door-to-door with volunteers, the reception was sometimes cold. "Baby killer!" one homeowner shouted as he slammed the door on her face.[8] Mulligan tried not to take the abuse too personally. Still, she was beginning to get a taste of just how nasty the campaign might become.

The first response of most people knocking on doors is to spend as much time as possible convincing every person you meet to cast their ballot in your favor. Some candidates waste hours at doors or during events convincing otherwise immovable voters about their side of an issue. But running for office requires turning off the understandable human instinct of being affirmed. It takes time for a candidate to learn that, despite however reasonable they may believe themselves to be, some voters simply won't be swayed.

For campaign staff, the typical duties often entail far more than just door knocking, getting voting literature out to voters, and running phone banks. One morning, Terry Cosgrove received a call at 5 a.m. It was Mulligan, and she informed him she wouldn't be able to make it to the events the campaign had planned that day because there was a raccoon stuck in her living room fireplace. So Terry Cosgrove got up and drove from his Chicago apartment in the wee hours of the morning to help lure the pest out of her home. During an intense campaign, the job descriptions are loose, and duties are often performed on the fly. Campaign staff gets done what has to be done, even if that means getting a raccoon out of the candidate's chimney.[9]

Most legislative campaigns don't garner much media attention because of their local nature. But the battle in the 55th District was being closely watched as prochoice groups began pouring vast sums of money into the district to defeat Pullen. State, local, and national media were paying attention. Because of this, coverage in the newspapers, on TV, and on the radio came easily. When a press release went out or the campaign called a press conference, reporters flocked to it like flies on manure.

The local press also played an important role in covering the campaign. Today, substantive coverage of state and local campaigns can be hard to come by. Year after year, small and medium-sized news outlets continue their sad descent into shells of their former selves. Nearly 200 counties in America today have no newspaper at all. Half of all counties today have only one newspaper—mostly a weekly publication—that is no doubt getting thinner and thinner with each passing edition.[10] But in 1990, the coverage of state legislative campaigns across the country was incredibly substantive, with at least seven local papers covering the Pullen-Mulligan race on a weekly basis. Not to mention, national media was keeping a close eye on what had long been billed as a post-*Webster* proxy war.

On one occasion, the Mulligan campaign decided to hold a press conference addressing Penny Pullen's record on children's issues. They sent out a press release announcing the event and released a four-page summary of her votes on drug abuse, education, childcare, and more. On many of the bills, Pullen was one of the only members voting nay, something Mulligan's campaign thought left Pullen vulnerable and illustrated how she wasn't representing her constituents. With media gathered around, Mulligan grabbed the mic and attacked her opponent from the podium. "The voters should know that our current state representative was one of only two in the entire House to vote against a bill requiring that school bus drivers be tested for drug and alcohol abuse before receiving their school bus driver's permits," she said to the crowd.[11]

While that was technically true, the attack was illustrative of other allegations she would level against Pullen that often clouded a more complex reality or left out important context. Pullen later explained that she voted against the bill because she believed random testing of bus drivers would be more effective as opposed to a one-and-done approach that applied when someone got hired for the job. Not to mention, Pullen had voted on more than 35,000 bills by this point in her career, so the vote was a consummate exercise in cherry-picking. But in politics, if you're explaining you're losing, and Mulligan made sure Pullen had a lot of explaining to do.

The campaign combed through Pullen's campaign finance reports to see if there was any ammunition that could be used to continue their offensive. They discovered she had taken a $250 donation from Sandoz Crop Protection, a company that had recently been in the crosshairs of federal authorities for allegedly improperly handling cancer-causing agents in their products. Pullen brushed the attack off when she caught wind of it. "I don't run a search-and-destroy investigation on every business in the 55th district to determine if Rosemary Mulligan thinks they're worthy," she told the *Chicago Sun-Times* when asked about the allegations.[12] Mulligan's campaign attacked Sandoz in a mailer with just days to go before Election Day. It caught the eye of the corporation. The company was not happy with being used as political fodder and said the allegations painted a false impression of its environmental record. So Sandoz sent two suited men with a cease-and-desist letter and a hammer to nail it to the door of the campaign office. When they arrived to find a metal and glass door at the office, the Sandoz representatives playing temporary henchmen decided to suspend with the drama and handed a letter to the campaign manager instead.

Mulligan was in the office at the time and was incensed by the threat that her campaign might be sued. She informed the lawyer that everything they were saying was true. Her training as a paralegal gave her the confidence to speak on the issue. "Feel free!" she shouted in response to a threat of a lawsuit.[13] Not easily intimidated, Mulligan informed them that everything at issue in the mailer was public record and they were merely pointing out the company's abysmal environmental history. The campaign never heard from Sandoz again.

• • •

Media coverage of both candidates often focused on their personal lives—that Mulligan was the twice-divorced mother of two; that Pullen was a never-married single woman now in her forties. "Is it difficult for a woman in public life to have a social life and survive both as a mother and a wife and as a politician?" the anchor of *Chicago Tonight* asked Pullen during an earlier interview, emphasizing her status as a bachelorette. "Well, I'm not a mother and a wife. I think that to some degree that's an advantage in terms of my ability to use my energies more full-time than if I did have a family to care for," Pullen noted defensively.[14]

Whatever Pullen or Mulligan thought of the local focus on their personal lives, it had little bearing on how the national press would cover them. Their race was a proxy war on abortion, and no matter the subjects the candidates tried to run on—roads, property taxes, education—that hot-button issue dominated. "If they want to make this a litmus test, they may regret it when the votes are counted," Pullen insisted.[15]

Just a few days before the March 20 primary with the office teeming with volunteers, a *Los Angeles Times* reporter came to Penny Pullen's office to interview her about the race. Pullen had previously experienced plenty of national attention during her appointment to the AIDS commission, but the amount of coverage devoted to this reelection campaign was a first. Before Pullen greeted the reporter at the entrance to her headquarters, a woman jogged down Talcott Street just past the campaign office and paused long enough to flash a middle finger before continuing her run. At this point, it was impossible for the average citizen in the district not to know the area was in the throes of a heated campaign, and most voters had already developed strong views about the candidates. "I'm not running for national office, I'm running for state representative in this district," Pullen told the reporter, downplaying the race's significance.[16]

Pullen also continued her attempt to minimize the importance of abortion on the race. But while she did so, supporters continued to gather at Lutheran General Hospital and sing her praise. "Of all the candidates I've ever known, she's the one glowing light who hasn't run from the issue," someone said of her while marching outside the hospital holding a picture of a red rose imposed over a fetus.[17] Pullen wanted to discuss other issues, but that became tricky. Some of Pullen's most ardent supporters were with her strictly because of her position on abortion and cared little about her record on local issues. This required Pullen to walk the fine line between remaining strong in her prolife views when speaking to activists while not appearing too rigid with undecided voters who might not share this priority.

Aside from some staffers sent by Republican leadership, Pullen mostly relied on the help of friends and her state office staff who volunteered their time. In Illinois, state employees are not *required* to help out with their boss's reelection campaigns, but if they know the meaning of job security, they do it anyway. Mary Schurder, Pullen's loyal state office administrative assistant, transitioned to the campaign, working tirelessly for the effort and serving as a fruitful source for local volunteers. Above all, Pullen wanted people around her who she could trust.

One of Pullen's old friends, Mike Jakcsy, was hired to be the face of the day-to-day campaign. Jakcsy was a man who wore many hats—a former teacher, an attorney, a pastor, and a management consultant to boot. When it appeared this campaign would require more work than her usual races, Pullen asked him to help keep things running efficiently. Despite any titles, though, no one questioned that Pullen was the one calling the shots.

Other staffers sent by House leadership in the final weeks of the campaign oversaw some of the volunteer operation and made sure her mail got out of the office on time. Despite being flush with cash, it was a frugal operation, something Pullen insisted on. Instead of hiring an expensive vendor to handle campaign mailings, staffers would stay up into the night printing out labels and hand-sorting and bagging the mailers by zip code. They'd bring the pieces to the post office and ship them out via third class mail. The staff also managed the day-to-day with volunteers who helped knock on doors, make phone calls, and lick envelopes whenever needed.

Pullen continued to enlist big names for help in February and March of 1990. Former Alabama senator Jeremiah Denton, well known for his conservative stances on social issues and his time spent in grueling captivity as a POW during the war in Vietnam, flew in to support Pullen, with whom he shared an ideological bond. Congressman Henry Hyde, conservative hero and saint of the prolife movement, endorsed her at a fundraising brunch. He gave an impassioned speech about how voters needed Pullen in Springfield to continue her great work. The campaign bought advertising in all the local newspapers the week before the election that featured a letter signed by Congressman Hyde. The election provided voters "a unique opportunity to affirm an outstanding public servant," he wrote.[18] Pullen thought Hyde was a consummate public servant, and his many terms in Congress solidified her opposition to term limits, an otherwise popular proposal for most voters.

In Pullen's view, if the voters wanted to send a representative back year after year, it was their prerogative. Many of the other mailers included Pullen's national work and featured her with Ronald Reagan and George H. W. Bush. Experience was Pullen's asset. Mulligan was a lightweight, campaign literature asserted, while Penny Pullen was a political force to be reckoned with.

As always, the media continued to focus on the issue of abortion, but the campaign tried to keep things positive and locally focused. "This has been an issue in campaigns for years and I've been elected seven times," she told a *Chicago Tribune* reporter. "The poll that really counts is the one that's taken on Election Day." Pullen's campaign targeted conservative voters, prolife supporters, and niche constituencies for whom she had sponsored legislation, such as local business leaders or boating enthusiasts facing tighter licensing requirements.[19]

Mulligan's mailers, on the other hand, were much more aggressive. One piece that went out to voters, "Penny Pullen's 10 Worst Votes," listed ten votes on which Pullen had mostly stood alone. The campaign shrewdly listed the bill numbers and dates to lend the piece greater credibility. The mailer also discussed Pullen's opposition to the bus driver drug-testing bill and claimed she wanted to "give a rapist the right to prevent his victim from seeking an abortion." Pullen was easy on sex offenders, had a soft spot for criminal daycare workers, and voted herself a pay raise, the mail piece claimed. It concluded with a call to action to voters. "Pick your favorite!" it read, encouraging voters to pull out a piece of the mailer and send it to Pullen's state government office. Many voters followed suit and flooded the incumbent's mailboxes with sometimes nasty comments. The mailer shocked Pullen and her team. On one mailer sent to the office, a potential voter expressed his trepidation about her record in a handwritten note. In pen, he circled the votes listed on the mailer that concerned him and pleaded for clarification. "I was going to vote for you, but now I don't know. Are these really your votes?" he asked.[20]

The mail piece infuriated Pullen's campaign. They felt it left out important information that would have given context for the votes and was a cheap political stunt unbecoming of someone wanting to serve in the legislature. So Pullen drafted a detailed response in a letter to all her precinct captains explaining each vote, one by one. Her campaign wanted to make sure their surrogates were armed in the field with proper responses to the unfair attacks.

Pullen wrote many of her mail pieces, continuing to reject the help of campaign consultants who she thought were overpriced and a waste of money. For candidates who spend hours and hours raising funds, it can be a soul-crushing experience to see your hard work quickly devoured by high-priced consultants. There are consultants for mail and TV ads, those who write copy and provide policy advice, and communications experts who will help place op-eds and conduct media training. Some are paid hourly, some are on retainer, and others are compensated based on a percentage of funds they spend, a custom that is hard for a newcomer to fathom.

Many consultants are hardworking. Others are grifters. The reality is that political consulting is not like regular consulting. To be sure, there are metrics—the number of views on an ad, dollars raised at an event, mailboxes stuffed with literature—but the profession is more art than science. Some consultants make a living from being in the right place at the right time. Winning one important race can serve as the proverbial golden ticket for a political professional. Those with a stellar record can make the case to candidates that if they pay them enough, a victory can be delivered. But what many consultants conveniently forget or purposely choose to hide from their clients is that much of the result is out of their control. When a candidate wins—or loses—it often has more to do with the makeup of the district in which they're running or the partisan wave that's coming because of the popularity of the person at the top of the ticket. The cake is mostly baked before a candidate even decides to set the oven. Jesus Christ himself could run for office, but if he doesn't have the right party ID next to his name on the ballot, winning a campaign in the wrong district will prove harder than turning water into wine.

Following the fury caused by the continued misleading attacks put out by Mulligan's campaign, Pullen pressed on. "Penny Pullen has a record—and it's one we can be proud of!" another advertisement in the local paper proclaimed along with a picture of the smiling candidate. Yet while the campaign kept reminding voters just how effective their state representative had been in passing legislation down in Springfield, Pullen's most zealous supporters, again and again, inadvertently undermined her message.

In one of her final pieces with the March 20 primary just days away, Pullen spoke about taxes and spending. Immediately next to it, the Illinois Federation for Life ran an ad with a picture of a nineteen-week-old fetus in the womb and the words, "When they tell you that abortion is a matter between a woman and her doctor, they're forgetting someone." Try as she might, there was no diverting voters' attention from the real issue on the ballot.[21]

Rosemary Mulligan chats on the phone in her Park Ridge campaign office during the heated campaign. Photo Credit: *Chicago Tribune*/TCA

8

GOTV

I told you I'd beat that bitch!

Political campaigns are like startups. Workers toil tirelessly seven days a week in the leadup to an election or a product launch, with a one-track mind toward a common goal. Sleep is a luxury, and so is any semblance of a divide between work and personal life. New hires flock to their employer because of the leader at the top, sometimes learning later the figurehead's carefully crafted image is all a façade. In Silicon Valley and in Washington, prickly personalities are frequently rewarded over those with a cool demeanor. Novices just entering both fields come with naïve visions of changing the world and usually end up settling for a comfortable career instead.

Political campaigns are also *nothing* like startups. Instead of stock options with the potential for cashing out millions after an IPO, campaign workers usually earn a pittance. Some nascent companies are known for their trendy offices and progressive work environments; political staffers are lucky to have functioning internet and health insurance. When a business succeeds, there is room to grow and profit to be made. When a campaign is finished, it's time to look for another job. This is the industry that elects our leaders.

Luckily for Penny Pullen and Rosemary Mulligan, the heated nature of the race provided enough fuel to keep everyone going. It also provided motivation to keep the money coming. Elections in the Chicagoland area had always been expensive, and getting the message out required more than just pocket change. But the amount of money that was raised in the 55th District—especially the money coming from outside the district—broke records. By election week 1990, the campaigns combined had raised over $350,000, an unprecedented amount for legislative races at the time.[1] Much of that sum came from groups on one side of the abortion debate or the other.

For Pullen, PAC money continued to be a particularly fruitful source, including checks from the National Rifle Association, Philip Morris, Coors, Commonwealth Edison, and prolife groups. PAC money is often maligned as a tool for special interests to buy off politicians, but these groups present a chicken-or-egg scenario. Do PACs donate to candidates because they agree with the views the candidate already holds? Or do candidates hold those views because they receive PAC donations? Either way, both parties are rife with PAC dollars, some donations more transparent than others. Certain candidates, especially progressives today, make a distinction between *corporate* PACs and membership-based PACs, a line in the sand that means they're perfectly willing to accept donations from trade associations or labor unions, some of the most powerful interests in politics. When the money's coming from your side, sometimes it's simply too hard to turn down.

As Election Day drew closer, Mulligan continued speaking at events and making her candidacy known in the district. For weeks, hundreds of volunteers on both sides canvassed the district by knocking on doors, handing out literature, and reminding voters about the upcoming election. While Mulligan may have had a disadvantage with money, there was no shortage of enthusiasm from her volunteers to make up for the gap. Many of them came from Chicago—people Pullen deemed "lakefront liberals"—and were driven principally by their hatred for Mulligan's opponent. Although Mulligan's team insisted decisions were made locally and there was a strong base of support in the district, the campaign was in no position to turn away anyone willing to help.

It was the weekend before Election Day and about 300 volunteers gathered for a get-out-the-vote (GOTV) training in a local church basement. The campaign had recruited hundreds of people to work polling places, hand out palm cards to voters, and remind people to get out and make their voices heard that upcoming Tuesday. The crowd of volunteers was gathering to be instructed on their tasks when Rosemary Mulligan appeared among the sea of faces. Terry Cosgrove was befuddled. He walked toward her, pushing his way through the mass of people, and pulled her aside to another room. "Why are you here?" he asked her. Mulligan was confused at the question. "Well, it's a meeting of my campaign," she replied. The problem was, Mulligan's presence was actually quite unnecessary, and Cosgrove explained to her that she should be out knocking on doors and meeting voters. There was no work for her here, and with so few precious hours left on the clock, she should be making the most of her time.

Mulligan wasn't having it. "This is my campaign and I'll dammit be here if I want to!" she insisted. Cosgrove decided it was time to be clearer. "If you lose this election by ten votes then it's all your fault because you have absolutely no role here and your job with seventy-two hours to go is to go out and knock on doors and meet voters," he yelled. Mulligan picked up a packet of campaign literature and threw it at him. "You smart ass!" she yelled, proceeding to storm out of the building. She was pissed off, yes, but in the end, Cosgrove succeeded in getting her back out to knock on doors and meet voters.[2] Mission accomplished.

• • •

Many people think Election Day is the busiest day of the year for a political campaign. For many months, countless hours are spent preparing for a single event. The date has been marked in the calendar, circled, and counted toward with nervous anticipation. For the candidate and her staff, the day has been the absolute center. For everyone else, it's just another day.

Once that time arrives—if all has been planned right—Election Day should actually be one of the *least* busy days for campaign staff. Volunteers come in to collect their materials, but the work is mostly done. There are no more supporters to be recruited, events to be planned, or volunteers to wrangle. Election Day is like the period between when a bowling ball leaves your hands and before it hits the pins. While it's rolling down the lane you can do a lucky dance or yell with encouragement, but the final result is now out of your control.

The days leading up to this period are also both mentally and physically exhausting, especially knowing a period of rest is just within reach. It's akin to the final minutes of fourth quarter in a basketball game, with players groggy and leaving it all on the court. It's akin to the time immediately before a final exam, cramming in one last look at your notes before tucking them away and putting pen to paper. It's akin to the final hours of a long shift before a vacation, keeping it all together for the boss before you can let loose.

In the leadup to Election Day, campaigns and news outlets obsess over polls. Who's on top? Where is the race headed? And who's still undecided? There's no barometer for measuring how campaign staff feel about the race, but if given the choice between extending the race another month with the possibility of winning or putting it all behind for a day off and losing tomorrow, your average campaign staffer would probably choose the latter.

The early hours of Election Day can also inspire some last-minute confidence in teams. Every voter you speak to who says they're switching sides, each yard sign seen in a prime location, or even the anecdotes heard from out in the field, no matter how trivial, provide indications of how the day might be going. Even the weather can be cause for celebration, such as a rainy forecast over a less favorable side of the district or snowy conditions that might cause your opponent's geriatric base to think twice before leaving the house that day.

As the morning progressed and it became an appropriate hour to begin calling voters, the phone banks kicked into action. Phone bankers and political canvassers must be constantly sensitive to the voters they're trying to reach. Call too early in the morning and you might just peeve that person enough to decide to stay home. Call too late in the evening and you risk waking up a voter's slumbering children who they've just gotten to bed. If you catch a person while they're gathered around the family dinner table or headed out the door, chances are you won't have much success in bringing them to your side. Sundays are often sensitive times to call Christian voters enjoying their sabbath, while knocking on doors during Rosh Hashanah or Passover in a Jewish neighborhood might cause more harm than good for your candidate. The American electorate already loathes politicians, so campaigns must avoid any unpleasant contact outside the usual poking and prodding.

March 20, 1990, had a forecast of clear skies and a high of 45 degrees, and Pullen's team was feeling confident. The campaign team set up a victory party at a local banquet hall and had it catered. They were ready to reward volunteers for their hard work and celebrate the primary that would secure Pullen an eighth term. Pullen spent most of the day at home preparing for the election night party. She caught up on some work, washed her hair, and laid out her clothes for the evening.[3] When the race began months before, she hadn't given Rosemary Mulligan the time of day. She knew now that the results would be closer than anticipated, but victory was still forthcoming. With the polling places nearing the final hours, Pullen made her way to the victory party and settled in to watch the results.

Pullen and the team stayed huddled in a back office for most of the night, paying close attention to the numbers as they rolled in. Most campaigns worth their salt set aside a "war room" where the staff like Mary Schurder, Mike Jakcsy, and others gathered to analyze results in real time. Some campaigns prohibit the candidate from being there and adding stress to an already tense atmosphere. But Pullen was in charge of her operation, not a hired gun, so she sat along with her confidants and dissected the returns. One by one, poll watchers would phone in the results that staff would record in a spreadsheet. In the age before the internet, gathering results was a laborious process that required humans to grab paper tapes that printed out from voting machines and report them back to the campaign. Today, a campaign might send someone down to a county office for some advance notice, but the results are mostly put online with little delay. War room activities are a silly exercise for most campaigns given the result can't be changed once the polls are closed. But in the event of a close race or another mishap, having the correct data at your fingertips will keep your team one step ahead of the opponent.

The polls closed at 7 p.m. and results began to come in from all 114 precincts across the 55th District. The Pullen team waited with anticipation for the first set of returns. When they finally arrived, confidence quickly turned to unease. Initial tallies showed Mulligan and Pullen virtually tied, something that was an early disappointment for the hopeful team. As the night rolled on, the rest of the district showed a similarly close race. In the other room, supporters chatted away and awaited word of what they thought was an impending victory. After some time without news, the mood began to darken.

Shortly before midnight, Pullen left the war room where her staff and family were gathered and began hugging supporters. She announced to the crowd that she was going to await the remaining results from home. The counting had slowed, and it appeared it was going to be a long evening. For the first time that night, Pullen had pulled ahead and was holding on to a slim lead of just nine votes.

Regrets began to flow quickly through her head. Had she taken the primary seriously enough? Had she been too bold? Not bold enough? This job was her life, after all, and losing to a primary challenger was not the way she wanted to go out. As supporters continued to commiserate, Mary Reilly led a prayer among those gathered at the party. She wasn't about to give up on victory.

• • •

The routine for Mulligan's team largely mirrored that of her opponent. The most dedicated volunteers arose at 5 a.m. to place signs at polling places across the district. Each received around a dozen assignments which they were to complete before the sun rose. After the early morning work was done, some members of the team met for breakfast with Mulligan at a local diner at 7 a.m. sharp. Many longtime politicians have a ritual they follow on Election Day. Barack Obama was known for playing a morning game of basketball with friends, for example. Mulligan's team was hoping this would be the start of their own ritual for many years to come.

The night before, an army of volunteers put out signs in other places across the district. Like most campaigns, there was a mad dash to get them out the door. With just a few hours left until the polls opened, they'd have little use sitting in the office. In addition to election judges who sat at precincts and helped facilitate voting, the campaign stationed individuals at each location to hand out palm cards as people walked in the doors to cast their vote. It was the last chance to convince voters they should dump their incumbent representative and choose change. For a candidate who knew little about running for office when she began mere months ago, Rosemary Mulligan had come a long way.

Mulligan's brother Stephen Granzky had volunteered his time where he could over the past few months. A local English teacher, he had a family of his own to raise but still felt the need to be engaged. On Election Day, he was stationed at Lincoln Junior High School handing out palm cards to voters as they walked in to cast their ballot. One man approached the doors of the polling place as he noticed Mulligan's brother handing out literature. The man yelled at him, saying that instead of a campaign button Mulligan should be "wearing a swastika." His sister was not a Republican, the man asserted, she was a fascist who should be running under "the Nazi party because she advocates genocide." Until the very end, tensions were high.[4]

One poll worker handing out palm cards for Mulligan was pleasantly surprised at what she heard from an elderly couple who approached her as she attempted to hand them information. The couple informed the volunteer that they were lifelong Democrats, but for the first time in fifty years they would be pulling a Republican ballot and voting for Rosemary Mulligan. Another woman outside the polling place agonized over whether to vote in the Pullen-Mulligan race or the Democratic primary for governor. She stood outside, contemplating for about fifteen minutes before entering. When she emerged from the polling place outside, she told the poll worker that she made up her mind and voted for Rosemary Mulligan.

In their typical thrifty fashion, the Mulligan campaign threw together an election night party in the office instead of renting an event space. The crowd was slow to build because most of them had been out working the polls. Volunteers brought in chips and dip, pizza, booze, and snacks for people to feast on as the numbers rolled in. Results were released steadily after the 7 p.m. closure but slowed to a crawl around 9:30 p.m. The polls had only been closed for ninety minutes, but the habit of checking results nearly every minute made time pass slowly. Some of Mulligan's supporters began to grow nervous. "If we lose because of vote tampering, it stinks," an attendee remarked, echoing a constant paranoia that is innate in all

Chicagoans regardless of party.[5] Her supporters were suspicious already that the fix was in. Republican leadership was supporting Pullen, so they thought someone might be pulling some last-minute strings to bring her across the finish line. *What was taking so long?* they began to ask themselves. By 11:45 p.m., there was still no final answer.

As the final precincts began reporting their tallies, Mulligan finally pulled ahead. Her son Matt, home from college for the past two weeks, was by her side overdressed for the occasion in gray suit and red tie as she finally took the lead. People broke out in cheers at around 12:15 a.m. "31 votes! 31 votes!" they shouted.[6] With all 114 precincts reporting, she had pulled it off. Mulligan embraced her younger brother Stephen who was standing nearby. Supporters in the room began to cry tears of joy as others busted open bottles of André Extra Dry champagne and passed drinks around in paper cups. Even in victory the team was scrappy. As Mulligan approached the mic to address those still gathered on what was now technically the day *after* Election Day, she could barely contain herself. "I told you I'd beat that bitch!" she proclaimed to the crowd.[7]

A portrait of Judge Francis Barth in his chambers in the Circuit Court of Cook County. Photo Credit: Francis Barth

9

Dimpled Chads

Both sides of the abortion rights issue are studying the results of a significant vote in yesterday's Illinois primary, . . . and the deciding issue appears to have been abortion.

The headlines following Election Day were clear: "Mulligan the Winner by 31."[1] The final tally was 7,431 for Mulligan and 7,400 for Pullen. Around the district, reaction to the results was about as split as the vote itself. "She's been around so long," said Stan, an older Park Ridge resident, about Pullen. "Not enough people voted," said another. Walt, another local resident, was blunter: "I think the other one [Mulligan] was mouthy." Others had the same view on the vanquished: "I think [Pullen] was too opinionated. Her position on taxes was much too weak."

Residents also continued the trend of expressing divergent views on abortion. "I think the defeat does not reflect the abortion issue," said one local prolife voter, downplaying the significance of Pullen's loss.[2] But takeaways from the national media begged to differ on that conclusion. "Groups on both sides of the abortion rights issue are studying the outcome of a significant vote in yesterday's Illinois primary," said anchor Diane Sawyer on *ABC World News Tonight* the day after the election. "In a very close race, a longtime member of the state legislature was defeated in her bid for reelection, and the deciding issue appears to have been abortion." Coverage from other national outlets echoed that takeaway, treating the loss as a major victory for prochoice leaders.[3]

In total, the turnout in the primary was 6,000 votes higher than the previous year and was the highest turnout of any primary election in the district's history.[4] Pullen quickly attributed the victory to Democratic crossover and began penning a letter to her supporters pointing this out. Local Democrats vehemently denied any official involvement in helping to bolster Rosemary Mulligan, but there were rampant rumors that an effort was conducted behind the scenes. Either way, there was no denying that crossover vote from Democrats had influenced the outcome.

National prochoice groups took a victory lap over Mulligan's win. "It should send a message to every anti-choice legislator in America . . . that if you're out of touch, you're out of office," said Kate Michelman of the National Abortion Rights Action League. Prolife leaders disagreed, attributing the loss to Pullen's not making her views on abortion clear enough to voters. "The real message is that the pro-life candidate must be totally upfront on being pro-life and paint the pro-abortion opposition as the extremists that they usually are," insisted Dr. John Wilkie of the National Right to Life Committee.[5]

There was some regret among prolife groups in Illinois too. The Illinois Federation for the Right to Life approached Pullen before Election Day about running a series of newspaper and radio ads in support of her campaign, but the Pullen team thought any more highlighting of the abortion issue would harm her, so they asked the group to hold off.

Both sides of the abortion debate had invested a great deal into the race, and by March, 68 percent of Mulligan's contributions were from out of the district compared to 57 percent of Pullen's.[6] Neither candidate could claim her operation was completely homegrown.

Other individuals tried to claim credit for the win too. Groups as obscure as the Northern Illinois Chapter of American Atheists, with fewer than 100 members in the district, insisted they tipped the scales. The group's executive director accused Pullen supporters of being "zealots for zygotes."[7] The group was a nonfactor, to be sure, but had previously picketed Pullen's state office a few years earlier when she sponsored a resolution in the General Assembly for a "day of prayer for rain" during an extended period of drought in Illinois. "Two, four, six, eight, separate church and state!" nine nonbelievers had shouted outside her office.[8]

Within a few hours of the results coming in, it became clear to anyone paying close enough attention that a recount was in order. But it took some time for that reality to settle in for those more personally invested in the result. Pullen's team rejected any notion that her strategy was to blame. "Our literature went out and dealt with major issues of the 55th district, like taxes, flooding, and major road improvements she's brought to the district. She's been a strong anti-abortion voice. The voters already know that," Pullen staffer Tim Schmitz asserted.[9] Schmitz was dispatched by House Republican leadership to help with the campaign, a temporary assignment that many political staffers become accustomed to as an inconvenient but necessary part of the job. Schmitz and his wife had long planned a vacation to Phoenix, Arizona, to visit family once the race was finished. They counted down the days until Election Day, but once it appeared a recount was on the horizon, Schmitz knew his plans were shot. "There goes Phoenix," he told his wife on election night.[10] The end of a race can often be a relief that the campaign season is over no matter the outcome, but Schmitz recognized his work was beginning anew.

Penny Pullen spent the day after the election at home. She was fresh off an agonizing defeat and being flooded with questions about what went wrong and what she may have missed. Pundits, volunteers, journalists, and everyone in between began dissecting the results. But Pullen tried to tune out the attention. While reflecting on the previous night's events, Pullen was visited by one of her dear friends, Cal Skinner.

Skinner had served as a state representative alongside Pullen, worked on her staff for a time, and helped during her appointment to the Reagan AIDS commission. A political junkie at heart, Skinner was a conservative like Pullen but with a libertarian streak. At first glance, someone might confuse him for a thin version of legendary Cubs broadcaster Harry Caray. Just shy of fifty, Skinner was a tall man with thick-framed, square glasses who could usually be found neatly dressed and wearing a striped tie. He was a well-educated East Coast native with years of political experience under his belt, and Pullen came to trust him both on a political and personal level.

Skinner hadn't given up on the race. He thought it was too close to call and encouraged Pullen to challenge the results. Thirty-one votes was simply too small a number to throw in the towel. And at this point, there were already rumors of some discrepancies in the vote tallies. "You've got to get a lawyer!" he implored her. "You've got to recount this."

Pullen was upset at the loss and still surprised at the closeness of the race. The polls all along had not foretold this conclusion, and it came as a shock. But she knew her friend had a point. With just 31 votes separating her and Mulligan, Illinois state law entitled her to a recount. The process, however, required the help of a lawyer. "Well, okay," she said. "Let's talk about who." They sat in her living room strategizing and discussed their options.[11]

Election law is niche. The work is cyclical by nature; election cases come only in election years. When they do present themselves, the cases often pay very poorly and come with little upside other than some potential notoriety in political circles.

The conversation quickly turned to the few lawyers in the Chicagoland area with election recount experience. Pullen had forgotten the most obvious choice. Mike Lavelle, a Chicago attorney, was often referred to as the dean of Illinois election lawyers. "Of course! Why didn't I think of him?" Pullen asked Cal Skinner.[12] A former marine and native of Ireland, Lavelle was a charter member of the Illinois State Board of Elections when it was founded in the 1960s. He later served as the board's chair and was in many ways responsible for crafting much of the state's election law. He wasn't just familiar with election law, he wrote most of it. Lavelle had also served as chair of the Chicago Board of Elections for a decade and was intimately familiar with the processes involved in recounts. But for all Lavelle's experience in election recounts, there was one problem: he was a Democrat.[13]

Pullen knew Mike Lavelle from his various visits in Springfield over the years. Whenever he was in the capitol for business, he and Pullen would exchange pleasantries. They stood on opposite sides of the aisle, but it was worth a shot.

Pullen hurriedly tracked down Lavelle's number and worked up the courage to ring him. If she was going to fight this out in court, she wanted the best lawyer possible. When Pullen finally got a hold of him, his response was reassuring. "I was hoping you would call," he said.[14] Lavelle had decided to represent his first Republican candidate.

• • •

When Mulligan awoke the morning of March 21, the phone calls were nonstop. Interview requests were flooding in from across the country, from the *New York Times* to *NBC News*. Both candidates had garnered intense attention for the last five months, but suddenly the focus was all on Rosemary Mulligan. When she turned on the evening news that night, she would be greeted by images of her election night party broadcast to millions of Americans across the country. Winning an election like this was a life-changing event for any soon-to-be state legislator, but the attention focused on her only intensified the experience.

Local reporters wanted a scoop too. Madeleine Doubek, a reporter with the *Daily Herald*, came to the office to get an interview with Mulligan. But some things don't change—even in victory, and Mulligan was running late. So Doubek waited. And waited. After two hours, she finally got her interview with the candidate who succeeded at beating Penny Pullen.

Despite the excitement, the team knew very quickly that a recount was likely. The campaign enlisted the help of Mulligan's colleagues at her law firm Miller, Forrest & Downing to begin the search for a proper election lawyer. The team called around to nearly everyone they could think of. One of the first names that came to mind was, of course, Mike Lavelle. But he turned down the case. Little did they know he would eventually represent their opponent.[15]

In many cases, speaking with the other party in a lawsuit can be disqualifying for an attorney. If confidential information is disclosed by a potential client, it could get in the way of their effective representation and run afoul of ethics rules. But at this point, the chance any important information had been disclosed by Mulligan's team was highly unlikely. Both sides only knew what was publicly disclosed about the results in the media. The most likely scenario is that Lavelle simply was more interested in taking on Pullen's case. Unknown to the Mulligan team were Lavelle's views on abortion. While Lavelle was a Democrat, he was prolife.[16]

After an exhaustive search, the Mulligan team eventually found a law firm in the south suburbs of Chicago that was willing to take on the heated case. One of the few lawyers in the state with significant experience in election law, forty-two-year-old Burt Odelson took his first election case just six months after graduating from Chicago-Kent College of Law in 1972. Since then, he had cut his teeth working with candidates on both sides of the aisle. Taking on Rosemary Mulligan as a client meant going up against Lavelle, his longtime mentor. Years later, Odelson would also be dubbed the "dean of election lawyers" in Illinois.[17]

Both Southsiders, Odelson and Lavelle had remained close over the years and often found themselves on opposite sides of the courtroom. But like any good lawyers, they were used to the drill and understood that it was simply business. Together with his associate Mat Delort, Odelson began studying up on the case.

When news of the potential recount spread, reporters were back pursuing the story. Both campaigns quickly learned that there had been early irregularities in the initial count. Precinct 10, a polling place at the First Congregational Church in Des Plaines, had been counted twice, something that would have to be resolved in a formal recount. It was the sort of casual error that happens in many elections but typically doesn't matter unless the race is close.

Pullen made it clear to local media that she wasn't giving up. "One of my best supporters was in the hospital and later passed away," she explained to a reporter from the *Daily Herald*. "His wife told me that the next morning all he wanted to ask was, 'How'd Penny do?'"[18] For Pullen, it was another illustration about how such a close race could change at any moment. For others, it was a desperate rationalization for continuing on.

The first step in the recount process entailed conducting a "discovery recount." In the discovery recount, each candidate was asked to choose 25 percent of the vote to recount—or twenty-eight precincts. When a potential discrepancy was found, the ballot was set aside for further review. Whatever information was gathered at this step would be used by each team to argue for or against a full recount of all precincts. Following the discovery recount, Pullen's legal team filed a petition to contest the election with the Circuit Court of Cook County on April 19, nearly a month after the March 20 primary.

The first court hearing to determine whether a full recount would take place happened on June 20. Judge Francis Barth was chosen to oversee the proceedings. Barth had a stellar reputation among his peers and both legal teams respected him. He had been known to read opinions aloud into the record by memory in complete sentences. A native Chicagoan, he attended the University of Illinois at Navy Pier, finishing his degree at DePaul University where he also attended law school. After practicing law for a few years, Barth was appointed an associate judge of the Circuit Court of Cook County in 1975, then elected as a full circuit court judge in 1988. Barth understood the law, didn't care for political maneuvering, and was a straight shooter. He was a gregarious man with glasses, a square face, and black hair with nascent specks of gray.

Judge Barth was first tasked with considering the evidence that the teams had gathered during the discovery recount. Pullen's team had the burden of proving there was a reasonable likelihood the results of the election would be changed if a recount was held. With just a few votes separating them at this point, it was a low bar.

Mulligan attended the hearing and would continue that pattern for most court appearances. As a paralegal, she had an interest in the law and understood the process. She wanted to be engaged in the effort and understand the moves her attorneys were making. Pullen, on the other hand, found it unnecessary to attend and put her faith in her attorneys.

The attorneys made their arguments at the Daley Center in Chicago. During the discovery recount, Pullen's team had gathered that with the double counting error from Precinct 10 rectified, as well as a few other challenged ballots, they would pick up at least 25 votes in a full recount. "We have enumerated precinct after precinct with regard to the changes in result," said Lavelle. "We have asked that Penny Pullen be declared the winner."[19] Odelson, Mulligan's lead attorney, quickly countered in his opening statement. "If the result is not likely to change, it is not in your purview to order a recount," he implored the judge. "They must produce evidence now, not a fishing expedition, not a 'Let me have a crack at them now.'"[20] At each hearing, supporters packed into the courtroom to show backing for their favored side while reporters sat swiftly scribbling notes to recount the hearing for the outside world.

Judge Barth was skeptical of the argument not to proceed with counting all the votes. "It's clear to me from the evidence presented that this was not done in an attempt to corruptly influence the election. I can see no justification for disenfranchising the voters involved here," he noted from the bench.[21] After extensive back and forth, Judge Barth adjourned and both sides began anticipating his ruling. Every day that passed meant less and less time for the primary victor to prepare for the general election.

About a week later, on June 28, Barth came out with his decision. A full recount was ordered to take place. It was a huge win for Pullen and a massive setback for Mulligan. At that point it became clear the legal battle was nowhere near the end. Despite the disappointment, Mulligan was determined not to let the ruling weaken her resolve.

• • •

It was late on a Thursday afternoon when Pullen received the phone call. "We have our recount!" Bob Mankivsky, a member of the legal team, informed her.[22] She was ecstatic. It meant she had been granted another lifeline, and she felt right away she had made the right choice in picking her legal team.

Coverage of the recount quickly proved as intense as the election fight. Requests from national media continued to pour in. Pullen even filmed interviews live in Springfield between committee meetings. Every news outlet from CNN to ABC wanted to hear about the recount.

The procedure began early on a Monday morning at the Cook County Clerk's warehouse at 23rd and Rockwell in Chicago. Each day of the count, dozens of volunteers would be required to monitor the process as the nearly 15,000 ballots were sorted through again. Warehouses like these where ballots were stored had become a thing of folklore among Chicago politicos. The suspicion dated back to when Richard J. Daley supposedly delivered Illinois—and thus the presidency—to John F. Kennedy in defeat of then-Vice President Richard Nixon. Even in the 1960s, there was talk in Chicago of dead people voting, precincts with 100 percent turnout, and other nefarious election shenanigans. And as in the 1960s, there was little evidence in this case that proved any of this activity to be true. Still, the rumors persisted, and the long mythology of political mischief in Illinois weighed heavily on the minds of both sides. Because of this, both campaigns kept a watchful eye on one another.

Pullen volunteers were suspicious of the county staff who were counting ballots, believing them to be cogs in the Democratic machine who would spare no effort to oust one of the state's most prominent conservatives. Mulligan volunteers were equally skeptical of the county employees, believing that Pullen and Republican leadership in the House had a cut a deal with machine Democrats to deliver her a victory in exchange for something in return. Mulligan and Pullen shared very few qualities, but political paranoia proved to be one of the things these warring factions had in common.

The warehouse where dozens of volunteers would be relegated to spend many long days counting ballots was far from glamorous. The cavernous building was more than 100 years old with multiple levels and a scissor-gate elevator that required a human operator to function properly. Cobwebs in the huge, high ceiling were visible from the counting floor and hung above large windows, many of which were partially shattered and held together by silver duct tape. Large tables were set up with folding chairs on each side where the recount would actually be conducted. The dungeon-like atmosphere helped create a sense of urgency, as both sides quickly realized they wanted to spend as little time as possible in the warehouse. Compared to knocking on doors, witnessing the ballot count was like watching paint dry.

Attorneys for both campaigns supervised each campaign's volunteers and made sure they were following the proper rules. Stations were set up with counting machines and precincts would be called out one by one. Only the staff member from the county could actually touch the ballots, but they would hold contested ballots up in the air and flip them front to back for each campaign representative to see. More than anything, having volunteers at the tables was a way of showing the opponent you weren't giving in.

No improprieties were formally being alleged by either side. The process was mainly one of setting aside questionable ballots for Judge Barth to decide on later. Five precincts at a time, county workers fed ballots into machines as volunteers sat on opposite sides of the table monitoring. When discrepancies were announced, a volunteer would request that the ballot be set aside for a hand recount. Some of the ballots hadn't been punched through fully, but dimpled. The amount of dimpling varied as well. One ballot would have a deep dimple that someone could feel by brushing a finger over. Others could be discerned when held up to the light to see holes that the machines had failed to register at the polling place.

As with the court proceedings, Pullen did not appear at the recount. She felt she was in good hands and things were going smoothly. Mulligan, on the other hand, was fidgety. She would pace back and forth during the proceedings and chat with volunteers. The team brought in a cart with pop, juice, and snacks for volunteers to keep them sustained. After the first few hours, it became clear that Pullen was picking up votes as the counting continued. With the clock ticking, Mulligan became more and more nervous.

Shining attention on the recount was a good way to continue raising money, and Pullen took advantage of it. The team sent out requests in the mail to her Penny Pals explaining that funds were needed to help pay for the legal battle. Her attorneys were charging a standard rate, she clarified, but this process is a long one that requires significant sums of money. The campaign put together a press conference at Pullen's office in Park Ridge. Accompanied by her attorneys, Pullen explained to the media that it appeared she would gain as many as 25 votes from the full recount. When asked by a reporter for comment on the Mulligan team's confidence, Pullen dismissed it. "I don't have to account for what she says," she insisted.[23]

• • •

After counting for roughly a week, the recount process was finished and all 15,000 ballots had been accounted for. Along with the folding chairs and dusty tables, the ballots themselves were put back in storage with the exception of the disputed ballots. The next step required presenting the evidence to Judge Barth at a hearing and convincing him which ballots were to be counted and which were to be disregarded.

When the hearing day came a few days later on July 16, 1990, the mahogany-paneled courtroom was crowded with supporters from both sides. Mulligan was delighted to see about thirty prochoice allies sitting behind the bar whispering excitedly with one another. Bucking her usual trend, Penny Pullen was also in the courtroom. It was the first time since an earlier campaign forum the two women had been in the same room, yet the arguments being made were now entirely out of their control.

Judge Barth sat towering over those gathered from his seat on the bench flanked by the Illinois and U.S. flags. He had seen election cases before, but the number of people now seated before him came as a surprise. Quieting everyone down, he began the proceedings.

Mike Lavelle argued for the judge to consider a set of 39 ballots that had not been counted because voters had been unable to punch full holes in the cards with their stylus, a pencil-shaped tool voters used to mark their selections on the ballot. These ballots weren't counted because the machine didn't register them as marked on Election Day. Lavelle's argument, on behalf of Pullen, was that it shouldn't matter what the machine does but what the voter *intended* to do. "If the intention of the voter can be ascertained, the ballot should be counted," he told the judge.[24]

Election law is unlike other areas of the law. Constitutional law scholars have strong opinions about how our nation's founding document should be interpreted, a battle between originalism and a living Constitution. In tort law, there are lawyers who represent insurance companies and those who chase the proverbial ambulance, both with sturdy views of just how large a damages award should be. In administrative law, some lawyers think the federal bureaucracy is a zombie that continues to grow without end while others believe a robust civil service is a cornerstone of democracy.

In recount battles, however, there are basically no fixed principles. Years later, during the 2000 Florida recount, the team for Vice President Al Gore would make essentially the same argument as Pullen, a conservative with whom he shared no political views. On the Bush side, Rosemary Mulligan's attorney Burt Odelson would assist Republicans in arguing against counting dimpled chads in the Sunshine State. "Do you really think that Bush won Florida?" Odelson would be asked more than two decades later about his work for the forty-third president during a radio interview. "No," he replied soberly.[25] The difference, in Odelson's view, was good lawyering.

Dimpled chads, deadlines for absentee ballots, and most other areas of recount law have no ideological home. You argue what you argue because it will put your candidate ahead. Plain and simple.

Sitting near her attorneys, Mulligan thought back to comments she'd received from voters in the district. Dozens of people had come up to her around town since the recount. Some began to apologize for not voting or expressed their regret about not bringing their spouse or another friend to the polls to help close the gap. Nobody knew it would be this close, they'd explain. Mulligan would smile, thank them for their support, and express how confident she felt about the recount. Still, the thought of neglecting to shake a few more hands, knock on a few more doors, or call a few more voters to make the difference weighed heavy in her mind.

One by one, Judge Barth would open envelopes with ballots inside and allow the attorneys time to argue whether each individual ballot should be counted. Once he'd heard enough, Barth would rule. At one point, he announced to the courtroom that, in fact, he was not keeping track of the count. But like many in the courtroom, Rosemary Mulligan was counting. As the judge made various rulings in Penny Pullen's favor, Mulligan had a hard time keeping her thoughts to herself and would express her disappointment to those seated around her. "Oh, shit!" she'd say each time a vote was added to her opponent's tally.

Judge Barth continued ruling on the various sets of ballots he would count and which he would disregard. He rejected Lavelle's argument about the intent of the voter, holding that whatever the machine counted should prevail. He was not about to get in the game of guessing what was in a voter's head at the ballot box.

By 4 p.m., Judge Barth had reached the end of the pile. There were whispers in the courtroom as people watching realized what had just happened. Mulligan lost 30 votes, while Pullen gained 1. After hours of arguments, multiple court hearings, a brutal campaign, hundreds of thousands of dollars spent, and many days passed in a decrepit warehouse counting all over again, Judge Barth had reached a final result: 7,387 to 7,387. "Judge," Burt Odelson, one of Mulligan's attorney's remarked. "I believe we have a tie."[26]

Rosemary Mulligan holds up an Eisenhower silver dollar for the cameras following a coin toss at the State of Illinois Center on July 18, 1990. Photo Credit: *Daily Herald*

10

Heads or Tails

I don't give up.

The recount had been an incredibly formal process. There were rules about what to do with ballots, who could watch, and how long it could take. When the first lawsuit was filed, strict procedures had to be followed in order to ensure a fair case. But in the event of an election tie, the protocol proved to be much less formal. According to Illinois law, the candidates flip a coin.

Judge Barth set the coin toss for Monday, July 18, 1990, at 10:30 a.m. That morning, Mulligan went downtown to the State of Illinois Center, a massive glass-paneled state office building at the center of Chicago. In many ways, the building served as a second capitol building for the state. As she entered the building, television cameras from outlets across the country greeted her along with a crowd of supporters chanting her praise. The coin toss made the story even more irresistible for the media. Mulligan spoke with her supporters and shook hands before she and her attorneys walked to the austere conference room where the toss was to take place. When they walked inside, a coterie of reporters from *Newsweek* to the *New York Times* and nearly every Chicagoland outlet were gathered. The print journalists leaned casually against the eggshell white walls and jotted into their spiral notebooks while photographers and camera operators focused their lenses on Mulligan.

To quell any accusations of favoritism, a neutral third party was chosen to flip the coin. Theresa Petrone was an Italian immigrant who had become well known as an election expert serving in various capacities in Illinois government. She was recognized for her effort to include ballot instructions in multiple languages for voters and expand access to absentee voting.

Petrone began her career in politics as a Republican but switched to the Democratic party, out of admiration for the leadership of Chicago Mayor Richard J. Daley.[1]

The first order of business in the room was deciding who would choose heads or tails. Printed on two sheets of paper were both candidates' names, which were folded four times in a small square then placed into a hat. Mulligan's attorney Burt Odelson was given the chance to draw a name from the hat, and Mulligan was overjoyed when the sheet bearing her name was chosen. She would call the toss. Mulligan chose tails, which her son Matt told her the night before he thought was the clear winner. The toss would be conducted with a 1971 Eisenhower silver dollar.

Mulligan gripped the paper with her name on it as she stood next to her attorney and mentally prepared for the event. The media and onlookers cleared a circle and made way for Petrone to begin the toss. Surrounded by eager spectators, Petrone held the coin between her fingers and steadied herself. The curly-haired commissioner in her late sixties wore a long pearl necklace and a dress with a clashing color scheme that looked like it was borrowed from a production of Andrew Lloyd Weber's *Joseph and the Amazing Technicolor Dreamcoat*. Balancing the coin on her thumb, Petrone threw it up in the air before it came down on the gray office carpet as reporters zoomed in with their cameras in to see the results. Tails.

Mulligan's supporters erupted into cheers. "Everybody told us to go for heads, but we said it had to be tails," a beaming Mulligan with a characteristic white flower on her lapel said to the cameras. "It happened the way it was supposed to," her son Matt told reporters, exuding confidence in the next step.[2]

Mulligan tucked the coin away and vowed to keep it. "I'm going to save this coin," she said. "No matter how much debt I get in I will not spend this coin."[3] She was confident, explaining to those gathered around that she would either wear it around her neck or display it in her soon-to-be legislative office.

• • •

Despite the excitement around the coin toss, Pullen was much more mellow. She understood the toss was mostly an exercise for the cameras and a formality that would merely decide which party was the appellant and which was the appellee in the next court proceeding. Her sister Peggy thought losing the coin toss was actually a boon to the effort because it would put her supporters back on alert that the effort wasn't over. Either way, Pullen was still eminently impressed with her legal team. When the earlier tie was ruled in Judge Barth's courtroom, she was heartbroken. The process had been gut-wrenching, but Mike Lavelle wasn't just skilled at lawyering, he was good with people too. As they exited the courtroom after the tie, he coached her as she spoke with the media while still in a state of shock.

After the coin toss in July of 1990, the media attention intensified—and so did the legal costs. Pullen's team estimated the four-month battle would cost up to $100,000 in legal fees. She received small checks and large sums from her previous supporters. In direct fundraising appeals from prolife groups, supporters were encouraged to help the effort. It was an all-hands-on-deck kind of ordeal.

As news reached other parts of the country, Pullen received small-dollar donations from strangers to help. A teacher in Sitka, Alaska, sent money from her Sunday school class and a note saying they were praying for Pullen each week. News even reached Uruguay, and some prolife supporters sent a check in the mail.[4] To save money, Pullen closed her regular campaign office and converted her government office into campaign space. Mulligan, on the other hand, was still operating as if she was the successful nominee, and opened another campaign office before the recount was settled. Both women were preparing for any outcome.

The legal team had just three weeks to prepare for oral arguments before facing the Illinois Supreme Court. The highest court in Illinois accepted a direct appeal on this issue due to the pressing nature. The clock was ticking toward November, so the case couldn't wait to be resolved at the normal pace of the appellate court and state docket.

Lavelle tried to visit his family back in Ireland as often as possible. Before agreeing to take the case for Pullen, he informed her that he had already planned a family trip to County Galway that summer. Much to his chagrin, he would spend much of it finding fax machines and telephones in rural Galway and shuttling papers back and forth to prepare for the upcoming trial. The vacation was important, but so too was a case that the whole state was watching closely.

While the lawyers prepared for appeal, Pullen kept busy with state work. When she returned for session in Springfield during the recount proceedings, colleagues were surprised to see her on the House floor. As someone in House leadership, she was already a high-profile figure whose loss would have rung throughout the hallways of power in the state capitol. But the national coverage made the challenge even more important. When asked by a reporter about the race upon arriving back to the capitol, Pullen didn't hesitate. "I don't give up," she said, smiling.[5] A colleague asked her about how she was so calm during all the chaos. "Let me tell you about Jesus Christ, who is my savior," she replied. "Whatever happens is in his will, and I trust him."[6] Aside from divine intervention, Pullen also knew she had a lawyer she could trust.

The outcome was still uncertain, but Pullen kept up appearances by holding events for constituents and continuing to conduct constituent work for those requesting help with their everyday needs. On Memorial Day, she marched with a smile through Park Ridge alongside a group of supporters. She recognized that it might very well be her last march through the district.

Despite the heat she received during the campaign for her views on abortion, Pullen was unwavering. During the Illinois Republican Convention in Rockford that summer, even while it was unclear if she would prevail, Pullen sponsored a plank in the party platform that called for a requirement that minors obtain parental consent before having an abortion. Many of the Republicans at the top of the ticket were prochoice and wouldn't go along with something they thought was better avoided in a general election campaign. The measure eventually failed, but it was worth a try for Pullen. Party platforms are meant to be aspirational, and Pullen never stopped aspiring.

Throughout the whole legal battle, Pullen and her supporters also continued to pray. They gathered for fellowship meetings and asked for a quick resolution of this fight. But despite their pleadings, the battle was just beginning.

• • •

The Illinois Supreme Court has two chambers where it can sit to hear cases. One chamber is just steps from the imposing state capitol in Springfield. The other sits in an office building downtown Chicago. The Chicago chambers are rarely used, but the August 9, 1990, oral arguments for *Pullen v. Mulligan* were one of the rare occasions where it made sense for the justices to break tradition and swap their usual stately digs in Springfield for the convenience of the more modern, Chicago-based courtroom. Each side readied themselves at their respective tables as the justices looked out over the packed room.

"Our next case this morning is called 70870496, *Penny Pullen versus Rosemary Mulligan*, and the appellant may proceed," Chief Justice Daniel P. Ward said, directing Pullen's attorney Mike Lavelle to begin.[7] An Irish Catholic Democrat and former Cook County state's attorney, the stocky, seventy-one-year-old Ward was serving his final term on the state Supreme Court where he was first elected in 1966. The all-male panel of judges wore classic black judicial robes with their collars and tie knots peeking out above.

Oral arguments were carried live on public television and radio, a rare occurrence for state supreme court arguments. In lieu of attending, Pullen watched from a distance. Mulligan attended and sat among friends and family in the rows behind her lawyers. She understood this could be the end of the road for the campaign and was irritated it had come to this point. Still, Mulligan tried to keep a sensible view of it all. The last time she was sitting before the Illinois Supreme Court was during an appeal of one of her father's murderers. Losing a political race would be heartbreaking, but it paled in comparison to the actual losses she had already endured.

There were a variety of tedious issues before the court such as absentee ballots that were never initialed by an election judge or others lacking precinct numbers. The most important issue concerned 27 ballots that were partially punctured with paper chads that had not been completely dislodged by the voters. The machine had counted some and not others. Whether or not to count these dimpled chads—the largest set of outstanding votes—would determine the fate of each side.

Pullen was blown away by Lavelle while watching on TV. He made arcane, boring arguments seem crystal clear for even the legal layman. Watching from afar, she felt confident in her case. The pomp and circumstance of the state's highest court was not getting into her head. Pullen believed the law was on her side, and the rest was in God's hands.

As the fifty-five-minute-long arguments came to a close, Mike Lavelle was given a final chance to speak. Sensing his last opportunity to make an impact, he grew animated, with his voice booming throughout the chambers as he reiterated his strong disagreement with what the other side was asking the justices to do. "Our argument is that if the voter goes in and his stylus penetrates the chad, if for whatever reason his chad is not removed, that should not be attributed to a fault of the voter, that's a fault of the election officials for providing faulty ballot cards," he implored them with his voice just a notch below a yell. Within seconds, the sound of a call bell cut him off. The arguments were finished, and it was now up to the state's highest court.

Each side hastily gathered their papers back into folders and packed up their briefcases. With the press corps gathered outside, both teams explained again the arguments they'd just made and expressed optimism that the justices would deliver a victory for their side. Now came the waiting.

After the coin toss, Judge Barth had thought the *Pullen* case was now behind him. His in-laws had recently moved to Clearwater, Florida, and he and his wife figured it would be an opportune time for a beach vacation with their two kids to close out the end of summer. Whenever Barth left the state, he made it a practice to leave the telephone number for wherever he'd be staying in case any issues came up. The Barth family packed up their car and began the eighteen-hour voyage to the Sunshine State. On one of the first mornings of the vacation, Barth was sitting outside on the patio in the warm sun drinking coffee, doing a crossword puzzle, and still recovering from the long drive. His mother-in-law poked her head in and said nervously, "Frank, they want you on the phone . . . Supreme Court wants to talk to you," she said with her thick Sicilian accent. Barth put the phone to his ear. "Frank, how are ya doin'?" he heard on the other line from Daniel P. Ward, the chief justice of the Illinois Supreme Court. Ward and Barth had known one another for many years, and the now-chief justice had been Barth's criminal law professor at DePaul University where he had also served as the dean. "I'm fine, judge. I'm enjoying the week off!" Barth said, almost anticipating the news to come. "Well Frank, we just got done with *Pullen v. Mulligan*, and we're sending it back to you, and my question is: how soon can you get back to Chicago to work on it?" Still exhausted and not eager to break the news to his kids, the Barths again packed up their car and made a two-day trip back to Illinois.[8]

On September 13, the Illinois Supreme Court released its official order on the matter. They wanted Judge Barth to conduct visual inspections of each ballot in front of the legal teams and judge the disputed ballots based on the intent of each voter. He was instructed to segregate each vote according to his ruling and hand them over to the Illinois Supreme Court for the final reading.

Now back from vacation, Judge Barth began to conduct the visual inspections in his courtroom across the street. One by one he marked each ballot as either counting for Mulligan or Pullen. He was to deliver his findings to the clerk of the Illinois Supreme Court by Tuesday, September 19. As he went through the ballots, Judge Barth placed each one in an envelope. He then combined the two into one large envelope for transporting across the street to the Supreme Court and marked them accordingly. When the counting was finished, he sealed each envelope. Two guards—members of each legal team—walked them over to the Supreme Court room in the Michael A. Bilandic Building and handed them to the clerk of the Illinois Supreme Court.

On September 21, the Illinois Supreme Court announced its final ruling in the case of *Pullen v. Mulligan*. The court had eight essential findings, but the most crucial holding said that dimpled chads—to the extent a voter's intent could be determined—should be counted based on visual inspection if their intent could be determined by a reasonable certainty.

"Where the intention of the voter can be fairly and satisfactorily ascertained, that intention should be given effect," wrote Justice Ward. "To invalidate a ballot which clearly reflects the voter's intent, simply because a machine cannot read it, would subordinate substance to form and promote the means at the expense of the end."[9]

At the end of the opinion, the court did something rare. Legal opinions are known for their verbose nature and lack of clear structure. To the untrained eye, rulings are often couched in legalese and nebulous terminology. But on the last page, the court added a simple chart adding up the vote totals. Rosemary Mulligan had 7,386 votes to Penny Pullen's 7,392. Pullen won by just 6 votes. The race was over.

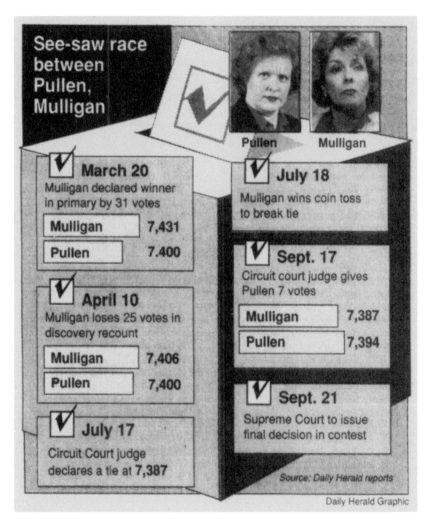

See-saw race between Pullen, Mulligan

Pullen   Mulligan

✓ March 20

Mulligan declared winner in primary by 31 votes

Mulligan	7,431
Pullen	7.400

✓ April 10

Mulligan loses 25 votes in discovery recount

Mulligan	7,406
Pullen	7,400

✓ July 17

Circuit Court judge declares a tie at **7,387**

✓ July 18

Mulligan wins coin toss to break tie

✓ Sept. 17

Circuit court judge gives Pullen 7 votes

Mulligan	7,387
Pullen	7,394

✓ Sept. 21

Supreme Court to issue final decision in contest

Source: Daily Herald reports

Daily Herald Graphic

A graphic in the *Daily Herald* explains the back-and-forth nature of the race. Penny Pullen's victory eventually came down to just 6 votes. Photo Credit: *Daily Herald*

11

Rematch

Pray for Rosemary, please.

"There's an old saying that victory has a hundred fathers and defeat is an orphan," John F. Kennedy once observed. In political campaigns, this statement holds even more true. Candidates are judged by a binary metric—either you win or you lose. Because of this, the winning candidate looks like a shrewd operator, and every move the campaign team made is analyzed for its now apparent efficacy. Every ad or mailer now looks smart. Each decision had a purpose. And the people who criticized the campaign suddenly discover a bout of amnesia erasing their past doubts. Everyone hugs the winner closer, like a hundred fathers claiming ownership of their political victory child.

When someone loses, on the other hand, the candidate is quickly dropped off in a basket on the proverbial firehouse steps. Gossip about the campaign begins to spread. Party insiders and self-professed political junkies swap *I-told-you-so's* to anyone who will listen. Campaign staff blame each other for not pushing harder. Pundits and political journalists point fingers about money being spent in the wrong place. Every tactical decision, even if it was the right call, is criticized with the perceived clarity of hindsight. A candidate can run the most effective, shrewd campaign since 1788 but if they lose, they lose. Nothing else matters.

For Mulligan and Pullen, the post-mortem of the campaign was a lot less clear than your standard campaign. Victory had come following a drawn-out legal fight, not an elucidating election night victory. Despite this, the win brought a great deal of relief to Pullen. What started out as a primary challenge she had hoped to quickly dust off became a saga displayed on the front pages of the Chicago papers and covered on national news. Throughout it all, she tried to keep her head down and focus her attention on her work in Springfield. No longer would she make the mistake of not taking a threat seriously.

After the announcement from the Illinois Supreme Court came down, Pullen and her team held a press conference with Mike Lavelle at her office. As they entered, about twenty supporters greeted her with cheers while reporters gathered around to ask questions. After months of work, it was a nice victory lap for the team.

"Pray for Rosemary, please," Pullen wrote in a letter to her supporters. "She doesn't have you with her; she doesn't have the support of love and peace." Whether intended as a jab or not, the comments only served to anger the other side even further. "We must take this opportunity to show graciousness and love," she continued. Pullen wasn't interested in courting Mulligan's support in the general election and never requested it.[1]

With only five weeks left to campaign until the general election, Pullen's staff and volunteers kicked into high gear. While Pullen and Mulligan were battling each other in courtrooms, their Democratic opponent had begun preparing. Robert Mucci knew the Republican infighting presented him with the best chance in decades to flip the 55th District. A thirty-six-year-old public defender for Cook County, he had kept a relatively low profile during the primary campaign. Mucci began conducting interviews with the local papers, building support with community groups, and most importantly, raising money. When asked by reporters about his platform, Mucci had demurred, saying he was waiting to see who his GOP opponent would be. Pullen didn't take kindly to his pussyfooting. She thought it was a sign of weakness. "You don't have to know who your opponent is to tell people in the district what you stand for," she said.[2] In the 55th District, the GOP primary was the real contest, and the Democratic race was a sideshow. But a protracted legal battle meant Democrats might have a shot at making the seat competitive.

Pullen's team had some catching up to do to finish the fight and pay off the campaign's remaining legal bills. The campaign held a fundraising brunch to celebrate her primary victory and roll out local endorsements. In the largest event they had held to date, more than 300 people showed up to express their support. Representative Henry Hyde attended and gave another full-throated endorsement of his friend and fellow prolife advocate. The local GOP committeeman and local elected officials also attended, along with Illinois House Minority Leader Lee Daniels. A sense of relief wafted over her supporters who, just a few months ago, were led to believe on election night that their representative's career had reached the end.

On Election Day in November of 1990, the general election in the 55th District was called with 111 of 114 precincts reporting their results. Pullen received 56 percent of the vote. It was a comfortable lead, but also her smallest victory since first being elected in 1976. The campaign chalked it up to Mulligan supporters helping the other side and failing to respect their party loyalties. "It's clear many of Mulligan's activists were working for Mucci—and she herself was too," Pullen asserted to the local papers.[3]

When she returned to Springfield, Pullen felt a sense of freedom knowing she had another two years in the legislature. The tight race didn't affect her sway, and she was renominated for a fifth term in leadership by Minority Leader Daniels. She had grown close to him over the years, and he understood the value of having her conservative voice at the table. Just a few years earlier, she had seconded his nomination for leadership. "Lee Daniels is indeed a leader. He respects us, he is sensitive to our needs," she proclaimed from her desk on the House floor.[4]

Pullen was welcomed back and congratulated on the reelection by many of her colleagues. The race had been the talk of the town, and she lived to tell the tale. She took a few moments on the House floor to thank the Illinois Supreme Court justices for establishing proper case law on the esoteric election issues that decided the race and for the "opportunity to receive justice." Pullen felt vindicated by the court. "It's good to be back," she told her colleagues from her desk, with the ornate chandeliers of the House floor hanging above her.[5]

The recount had been a stressful experience for everyone involved. Adding to that stress was the health of Pullen's father. Pullen and her father had a particularly close bond, in part due to their love of politics. Locally, her father had been involved with the township Republican organization and served as an alderman in Park Ridge. In the spring of 1991, he underwent two surgeries for prostate cancer all within a week. "He's at home, recuperating well, looking forward to feeling tiptop one day soon," she wrote in a letter to her Penny Pals.[6]

The year 1991 also marked a redistricting year. Based on results from the decennial census, legislative maps would be drawn to conform with shifting populations and other requirements. The Illinois General Assembly, which was controlled by Democrats, passed a bill that would lay out the map-drawing process. But the new Republican governor Jim Edgar swiftly vetoed the map. With the legislature unable to override the governor's veto, the process was punted to a commission. When the commission was unable to reach an agreement—likely the intended result for Republicans—a tie-breaking member was appointed. The chair of the Illinois Republican party was selected and cast the ninth vote on the commission approving new maps. Many of the changes were made in the Chicago suburbs, which reflected a population shift and an attempt to gain extra seats in the next election in favorable GOP territory.

The maps faced a series of legal challenges. At one point, the Illinois Supreme Court informed state leaders that if they didn't finish the process by January 6, 1991, legislators would be forced to run in at-large districts. Facing that threat of electoral chaos, a new map was finally put forth in January that met legal muster.

Like redistricting in many states, the process was an exercise in shameless political maneuvering. Republicans controlled this process for the first time in decades, because they had long been cut out of the decision-making by Democrats. In red states, legislatures carve up maps to the greatest benefit of the party both on the national and local level. In blue states, politicians are no more noble. Politicians are politicians, and where they can seek to solidify their power by wielding the tools of government, they will. In the last decade, many states have moved toward creating commissions to draw district lines in an effort to avoid partisan gerrymandering. Today, twenty-one states use some form of a bipartisan or nonpartisan redistricting commission. Illinois is not one of them.

After the maps were released, close political watchers began quickly analyzing the changes and what it would mean for the next election. In the 55th District—Pullen's—the northwestern corner of Des Plaines was taken out and Park Ridge was partly split across district lines. Local leaders were upset at the prospect of having the city divided in two and the confusion that would come with it. But aside from geographic changes that were made, there was one particular move that raised eyebrows: Rosemary Mulligan's house was cut out of the district.

• • •

During the hectic campaign, Rosemary Mulligan became used to the normal antics that came along with a heated race. The legal battle, however, was not something she could have prepared for. After coming so close to defeating someone she was told would be nearly impossible to beat, she was angry. "If we had a rematch today, we'd win," she told reporters following the announcement from the Illinois Supreme Court. "I am appalled by this decision. Being a lady, I will not say what I think."[7]

To others, Mulligan didn't hesitate to share what she thought about the whole process. She felt the election had been unfairly taken from her, and she wasn't about to just put it all behind her. Almost immediately, Mulligan vowed to continue the fight. "I'm definitely running again and I'm starting now," she told a friend after the loss.[8] For months, hundreds of people had put in hour after hour of work to defeat Pullen and in the end, it was all decided by a judge.

Some on the Mulligan team also thought there might be something more than just legal maneuvering that went on behind the scenes at the Illinois Supreme Court. The justices were elected officials, after all, and talk spread that a deal was reached among the justices and state Republican leaders that if they ruled for Pullen to win, Democrats could have a victory in the court in another case. It was a quid pro quo, they thought, and the justices were not immune to the political pressures faced by elected officials.

The suspicion stemmed in large part from the fact that on the day Pullen's legal team announced they would be appealing to the Illinois Supreme Court, Penny Pullen had a one-on-one meeting with Justice Howard C. Ryan, a conservative Republican on the court.[9] The Mulligan team had a hard time accepting this as a mere coincidence. To them, it was just further evidence of an effort behind closed doors to sabotage her insurgent campaign.

Pullen and Ryan did have a simple explanation for the meeting. Pullen had been appointed by President George H. W. Bush to the board of the Legal Services Corporation, an organization that provides legal help to those who cannot afford it. Justice Ryan was heavily involved with a group called the Lawyers Trust Fund of Illinois, and the two were set to discuss their mutually shared work. And in the end, Justice Ryan did exactly what was ethically required and recused himself from the election case. Still, the whole ordeal left a bad taste in the mouths of the Mulligan team, and they remained convinced there was a secret pressure campaign aimed at persuading the justices to follow their political hearts instead of their legal minds. "My sincere appreciation for your excellent, 'winning' work on my recount case," Rosemary Mulligan wrote to her attorney Burt Odelson on a plaque bestowed on him after the legal effort was finished. "I certainly had the better representation and case—hopefully, in the years to come, the real truth will come out."

Despite the hard feelings, dwelling on what may or may not have happened in the chambers of the Illinois Supreme Court wasn't productive for the team. "What's next?" Mulligan asked Odelson shortly after the loss. "How do we prepare?"[10] No tears shed. No time spared. The team discussed potential further legal moves, but decided it wasn't worth the fight. "I've gotten good press through this, let's just wait for the next primary," Mulligan said.[11] So Mulligan did exactly what she said after the loss and kept pressing forward. With nearly a year and a half to go before the next March GOP primary in 1992, Mulligan was ready to gear up for a rematch even years out. She returned to work at the law firm but continued holding events, staying in touch with volunteers, and keeping her name in the limelight. Being cut out of the district only angered her further.

State law allows candidates to run in adjacent districts, but the winner must move within one year. What might have been a difficult decision for your everyday candidate was a no-brainer for Mulligan. She was running in the 55th and if that meant selling the home in "Bonaguidiville" where she'd raised her boys, so be it. Mulligan felt the decision was a deliberate attempt by the powers that be to prevent her from running again. As Pullen was a member of leadership, Mulligan suspected she had a hand in carving her out of the map. The fix was in, she thought, and Pullen had clearly cut a deal with the mapmakers. This wasn't creative cartography, it was deliberate political gamesmanship. The process was well known to be plagued by backroom dealings where party heavyweights carved out their most favorable lines. But at the same time, some heavily Republican turf was taken away from the 55th District. In many ways, the map was less favorable to the more conservative Penny Pullen.

Candidates since the post—Civil War Reconstruction era have faced accusations of carpetbagging. When a politician runs for office in a place they're not from, opponents criticize them for not understanding the issues facing the voters they seek to represent. In a place with deep hometown pride, this can be a cutting and reliable attack on a candidate's credibility. But the culture and politics of adjacent state legislative districts are far less likely to deviate significantly than that of a completely separate state. Nevertheless, Pullen and her supporters made an early fuss in the leadup to the 1992 campaign about the potential for Mulligan running in a district she didn't even live in. So Mulligan got out front of the attacks by publishing a long letter in the local papers.

She explained that she had lived in the district for decades and her mother operated a business there when Mulligan was growing up. She talked about attending high school at Maine East. Mulligan described raising her sons in the area, how her family lived all around her in the district, and the activities she participated in as a resident. "I've lived in Park Ridge and Des Plaines since 1955 and that's the district I want to represent and where my supporters are," she wrote.

Pullen tried to coax her out of it, encouraging her to take a stab at running in her new district instead. "It would give her a much clearer and pleasant opportunity than taking me on would offer her," Pullen said.[12] It was an early warning sign that round two would be just as rough-and-tumble as the first.

Throughout 1991, Mulligan held early morning coffees to keep supporters engaged. When she could sneak away from the office for lunch or pack in time on a weekend, the team organized luncheons and events around different holidays such as a Mardi Gras fundraiser. Mulligan wasn't an elected official nor had she officially announced she'd run again for the 55th District seat, but she found a way to keep speaking to Republican women's groups and other community organizations. She knew the worst possible outcome of the loss was to be forgotten. Out of sight, out of mind. So Mulligan did everything she could to stay relevant during this downtime.

The Mulligan team held a fundraiser at Arlington International Race Course in August of 1991 nearly nine months before the March 1992 primary and with no official announcement yet made. First built in 1927 when horseracing was becoming a popular attraction, the park's 35,000-seat grandstand overlooked an expansive estate stretching over more than 300 acres of open land with an artificial pond at the center of the racetrack. Mulligan's guests gathered in the upscale Governor's Room that overlooked the track on a sunny day and sipped on cocktails as they watched the horses race by and made bets on the winners. During the main event, some attendees put their money behind a horse named "Miss High Hope" who won the six-and-a-half-furlong sprint at 1:19.3. The team was giddy at the symbolism and went down to the track to snap a photo with the jockey holding his medal after the race. Indeed, the race gave Mulligan and the team a bit of hope that this election cycle would be different. But just a few weeks later, the Arlington International Race Course contributed $500 to Pullen's campaign, the exact amount Mulligan's campaign had paid for the deposit on the room where they gathered. At this point, even horseracing had become political.

Eventually, Mulligan made the run official. "Penny Pullen asked her supporters to pray for me, stating that I lacked love and support," Mulligan said, taunting her opponent in an interview with a friendly *Chicago Sun-Times* political columnist. "Please be informed that their prayers have been answered. I have definitely seen the light and have decided to run again!"[13]

One of the campaign's first orders of business as 1992 drew closer was setting up a new office. After a brief search, the team found a location on busy Northwest Highway in Park Ridge. The office was not far from the old headquarters they had used in the previous race and just blocks from Pullen's state office. To kick things off, the campaign planned a weekend open house in November of 1991. Supporters gathered shoulder-to-shoulder in the office dressed in winter coats and gloves in preparation of the tasks ahead of them. Spread out across the tables was coffee and hot cider to keep people warm and energized, donuts for a quick bite, and blank petition sheets that each volunteer was to grab and gather signatures. By now, everyone knew the drill. Before sending the crew on their mission, Mulligan addressed the crowd and thanked everyone for their help. Red "Re-elect Mulligan" buttons were created for the occasion, paraphernalia that reflected the widely held view among supporters they had actually won the last election before it was taken away by the courts.

Throughout the two-day open house, a steady stream of faithful volunteers came in to grab petition sheets. Some volunteers took them home to family and friends while others stood outside busy grocery store parking lots and shopping centers in the frigid winter, pleading with registered voters for their autograph. Gathering signatures in any environment is difficult, but asking people to take their gloves off and scribble their name legibly while the Chicago cold stiffens their fingers only complicates things further. As sheets were brought back, a notary was on site to complete the process. Throughout the weekend, Mulligan continued mingling with volunteers and tried to keep people motivated. For the hardcore Chicago Bears fans, a TV in the back of the office carried their game against the Indianapolis Colts. The Bears won 31 to 17. Like Miss High Hope's winning race, a win for Mike Ditka and the Bears was another positive sign for the team.

Mulligan's son Matt graduated a semester early to help with the campaign as well, and she was comforted having him by her side. Despite her familiarity with fundraising after the 1990 campaign, Mulligan still dreaded asking people for money, so her son was tasked with keeping her on track with fundraising calls. Every serious candidate has "call time" where she dials through lists of donors and asks for an investment in her campaign, an exercise that often requires pushing the candidate to persist through the painstaking process. For Mulligan, call time was always a fight, so Matt sat with her for two hours a day while she made fundraising calls. After his mother hung up the phone, he took notes on the conversations and tracked each financial pledge. The process of call time is an awkward one for all those involved. The candidate is monitored like a teacher hunched over their struggling pupil's desk. Except the roles are reversed. Call time is the definition of managing up, where employees must supervise their bosses and nudge them along.

Abortion was again the central issue of the campaign and there would be significant outside support from both sides. Protesters continued to gather at Lutheran General Hospital as well. At one demonstration, nearly 1,200 people showed up and marched outside the hospital for three hours. The protest was one of four across the state and was less raucous than previous gatherings. A large group formed a cross along the streets surrounding the hospital in solidarity. The so-called "life-chain" was intended to be a silent demonstration reminding policymakers to find a peaceful solution to abortion. "It is an attempt to get more people who believe that abortion kills children to come out and draw attention to the problem in a non-threatening way," explained one of the organizers.[14]

National political attention was centered on abortion as well. The Supreme Court had agreed to hear a case about a Pennsylvania law that required women to undergo a waiting period and give their husbands notice of an abortion, and required parental consent from minors before going through with the procedure. *Planned Parenthood v. Casey* was expected to be a second opportunity for the court to chip away at *Roe v. Wade*, and it weighed heavily on the minds of both sides. The announcement by the court that it would hear the case was particularly worrisome for prochoice groups because Justice Clarence Thomas, a well-known conservative, had officially replaced Justice Thurgood Marshall, one of the court's liberal-leaning judges. The balance had shifted. That change concerned many of Rosemary Mulligan's supporters, and the campaign office had kept Thomas's contentious Senate confirmation hearings on during the early weeks of the race.

The *Casey* decision would eventually become arguably the most important precedent on abortion by upholding the core of *Roe* but allowing states more freedom in regulating the procedure. Written principally by Justice Sandra Day O'Connor, the *Casey* plurality opinion would eventually become the standard for thirty years until the Supreme Court overruled both cases in 2022 with *Dobbs v. Jackson Women's Health Organization*. After *Dobbs* came down, headlines splashed across TVs and newspapers proclaimed an end to *Roe*, but *Casey* was arguably the more important precedent at the time. Attention in 2022 also focused on the loss of Justice Ruth Bader Ginsburg on the court because of her legal work on women's issues. Legally speaking, however, it's the legacy of Sandra Day O'Connor that was erased in 2022.

The impending *Casey* decision made prochoice groups even more eager to support Rosemary Mulligan, but prolife activists hadn't forgotten about their friend Penny Pullen either. One of the earliest reminders of this for the Mulligan team was an older man who came to the office for weeks armed with a sign to protest Mulligan's prochoice views. The man would parade back and forth in front of the office with a giant picture of a fetus on a yardstick. Like a one-man picket line, he made his message unavoidable to anyone passing by. And while the volunteers for Mulligan often found the signs to be abrasive as they entered and exited the office, he mostly kept to himself. The Mulligan team kept to themselves too, focusing on the things they could control. The Supreme Court would have their chance to set a precedent on the matter that summer, but so too would the voters of the 55th District in the weeks to come.

Penny Pullen discusses pending legislation with fellow legislators in the Illinois House chamber. Pullen served as assistant minority leader for House Republicans. Photo Credit: Abraham Lincoln Presidential Library and Museum (Legislators Project by Mark DePue)

12

Talk of the Town

I'm afraid that in the campaign ahead, the Park Ridge police might be chasing homosexuals out of our woods and straight over to Ms. Mulligan's campaign headquarters.

For years, the *Des Plaines Journal* ran a section in the paper aimed at allowing residents to express their views on all sorts of issues. Its tagline made that point clear: "Exercise your right to free speech—24/7!" The "Talk of the Town" section became a main attraction for readers, and each week, residents from the area would call into the hotline and leave an anonymous voicemail. The messages were almost always entirely unedited when printed in the paper. In an age before social media, the section provided plenty to talk about.

"Talk of the Town" had always been known for printing colorful comments. In one instance, Penny Pullen was even criticized by a caller for wearing a fur coat at a local fundraising fashion show. No person and no subject was off limits for "Talk of the Town." So when two men were arrested for having sex in public at the local forest preserve, all hell broke loose.

"Call me homophobic, but given the upside down world we live in today, I'm afraid that in the campaign ahead, the Park Ridge police might be chasing homosexuals out of our woods and straight over to Ms. Mulligan's campaign headquarters," said one caller.[1] The comment echoed an attack levied against Mulligan by Pullen in 1990 that if she won, voters would see "gay pride marches through downtown Des Plaines."[2] It all stemmed from a speech Mulligan had given to a gay rights group during the last campaign. The issue was mentioned on and off in 1990, but it became front and center in 1992.

"My wife and I used to enjoy walks in those woods, but no longer. It isn't safe," said another fearful resident. Calls became increasingly violent. "Lock up homosexuals," said another irate Park Ridge reader. "I'm tired of hearing them blaming President Bush and others for not getting a solution to AIDS . . . put them on an island and they will die off eventually."[3] It was clear that callers were somehow blaming Mulligan for the incident in the forest preserve.

In public, Mulligan defended her past speeches before gay rights groups. The truth was, she hadn't been particularly active in supporting the gay community, but rather fell into the role. She attacked Pullen's record on AIDS because she thought her bills were nonsensical and failed to solve the problem. "She says she is protector of the uninfected, but I think she's on a witch hunt for the people who have AIDS," Mulligan told the *Chicago Tribune*.[4] When asked in candidate questionnaires from interest groups or responding to concerns from voters and reporters, Rosemary Mulligan would simply express her honest feelings about how she felt on things like civil unions and nondiscrimination ordinances. She hadn't viewed it as overtly supporting gay rights, she was just telling the truth. "We're going to be hit on [my support from gays who want to get rid of Pullen] anyway so we might as well be out front," she told one activist supporting her campaign.[5]

Penny Pullen was reviled in the gay community of Chicago, and the city's two gay newspapers, the *Windy City Times* and *Outlines*, began covering the race extensively. In each edition, political groups would buy ads in the papers encouraging readers to get involved. Pullen was so despised that in the *Windy City Times*'s first post—Election Day paper in March of 1990, Pullen's initial defeat by 31 votes was the publication's front-page story.

In mailers to supporters during the last campaign, Pullen had homed in on Mulligan's behind-the-scenes support from the gay community. "Their tactics—constant references to me in their newspapers, carrying my larger-than-life photo on posters in their parades, plastering my picture all over lampposts in their neighborhoods—are intended, I am sure, to intimidate me," Pullen wrote. The tactics, however, did little to deter her. "It seems that militant homosexuals are openly involved in Ms. Mulligan's campaign," the campaign wrote in a 2,000-word letter to supporters. "But what really motivates these militants to go after my political scalp is my leadership in trying to protect the uninfected public from the deadly scourge of AIDS." In Pullen's view, she was out to protect the public, and these activists were only getting in her way.

When news reached Chicago that Pullen would again be challenged by Rosemary Mulligan, many in the gay community turned out in full force.

Illinois's campaign finance laws required any contribution over $500 to be reported to the state upon receipt. This meant that instead of learning who was donating to your opponent's campaign each quarter, larger contributions became public knowledge more immediately. Sensitive of how Pullen might use their support, the gay community poured small-dollar contributions just under the threshold that would trigger automatic reporting to Rosemary Mulligan from addresses all over Chicago.

In a way, Pullen was inadvertently supporting the community too. One of her vendors disdained her past positions so much that he took the money the campaign paid him for his work designing mailers and donated it to the Chicago Gay Men's Chorus.[6]

While Mulligan's campaign was delighted to have an enthusiastic set of volunteers and money flowing in from the city, they understood she had to walk a fine line in a Republican primary. She didn't back down from her views or apologize for the speeches, but she did try to redirect attention to the local issues.

Still, the activity that took place in broad daylight at Dam No. 4 in the forest preserve continued to rile up callers to "Talk of the Town." They worried about joggers and the track team from the high school, which used the area to practice. They expressed concerns about the changing moral tide in a suburb with so-called traditional family values. And they made the jump to mass murder, too. "I just want to say thank goodness our Park Ridge police are arresting these perverts in our forest preserve. The thought of another Jeffrey Dahmer stalking in the streets of our community is too horrible to even think about."[7]

One caller had the audacity to suggest the problem was having two "dizzy dames" running as candidates for state representative, and he insisted it was time to put a man forth for state representative and end the drama. For him, it was an issue of hormones, not homosexuals.

There were callers who defended Mulligan too, making it clear that it was ridiculous to draw a connection between Mulligan's campaign for state representative and two strangers having sex in the forest. And yet, some callers continued to make the connection to serial killers. "I would suggest that anyone who thinks it's not a problem, read Terry Sullivan's book *Killer Clown: The John Wayne Gacy Murders,*" said a caller from Des Plaines.[8] In fact, rumors began to fly from the other side that Mulligan had started a legal defense fund for John Wayne Gacy who was then on death row following his 1980 conviction. With no more than a conspiracy mindset, they asserted she was supporting the country's most notorious serial killer with his legal troubles. Never mind that Mulligan still had legal bills of her own from the recount battle.

The Gacy rumor was particularly pernicious because his final victim had hailed from Des Plaines not far from where Mulligan and her family lived. Gacy himself had been involved locally just a few towns over as a Democratic precinct captain. To those who thought Mulligan was a Democrat masquerading as a Republican, it was easy to make the leap that the more socially liberal candidate must somehow be connected to the Killer Clown. At night, Mulligan and her son Matt would read the comments from the papers aloud and laugh at how ridiculous the race had become. "Wow, there's a lot of people that really hate you!" Matt laughed to his mother one night when flipping through the news.[9]

· · ·

"If they couldn't do it this time I have no qualms about 1992," Pullen confidently insisted after the first campaign to a local reporter about her back-to-back challenge. In her mind, there was no sense in running scared from someone she had already beaten fair and square. Sure, the race was close last time, but Pullen would be better prepared for whatever mud that was surely to be slung.

Pullen doubled her efforts this time around, and she doubled the size of her campaign operation too. In the early weeks of 1992, she began hiring more staff and opened two offices, one in Park Ridge that would serve as the home base and another in Des Plaines that would help her reach outside her comfort zone in the western part of the district.

The power of incumbency was a helpful tool for this campaign as well. As with any officeholder, garnering media attention is easier for those who actually hold office. In Congress, for example, more than 90 percent of incumbents are regularly reelected each election cycle.[10] Getting elected is hard, but losing your seat might be even harder.

Pullen used her incumbent status to announce state grants to the Lutheran Social Services agency in her district and a $240,000 grant to Maryville Academy, a local childcare nonprofit. She touted the legislation she was passing in Springfield and all the great things she was doing to keep the district front and center. And she held events for constituents—job fairs, ribbon cuttings, and award ceremonies for the local high schools.

Favors were called in from old friends as well. Phyllis Schlafly, the founder of STOP ERA and a conservative icon, wrote a fundraising letter to her supporters asking them to back Pullen's reelection campaign. "One of my dearest friends and our number one leader in the Illinois House is in great need of your financial and prayer support in winning re-election to her ninth term," she wrote.[11] The letter mentioned the groups that were supporting Mulligan and remarked that liberal interests were behind her. Pullen was rewarded for her fight against the Equal Rights Amendment by Schlafly's Eagle Forum group, which donated handsomely to her campaign. Representative Henry Hyde also drafted a letter supporting her that the campaign used in newspaper advertisements across the district. He reiterated how effective she was as a public servant and why he needed a friend down in Springfield.

Learning from her experience last time, Pullen also hired a professional campaign consultant out of Texas named Kevin Burnette to oversee the operation. Consultants on campaigns generally oversee the larger issues, like working with vendors on mail or TV ads and guiding the overall strategy of the race. For a campaign manager to run the day-to-day operation, she hired Jefferson "Jeff" Angers. Angers was from Louisiana and had been involved in politics in a variety of capacities. Pullen had met Angers through her work with the American Legislative Exchange Council, a national group of conservative state legislators, and he came highly recommended by leaders whom she trusted. Still, it was an interesting choice to hire out-of-state workers given the carpetbagger accusations that she had leveled against Mulligan for running in a district where she didn't live.

Campaign staffers shipped in from another state almost always face scrutiny from locals who view them with skepticism and a *you're-not-from-around-here* attitude. Party leaders, local campaign staffers, and elected officials like to think that each state and each district is so different that you have to be born there to *really* understand it. Their politics are unique. It's complicated. You just won't get it. But in reality, political campaigns are mostly plug and play. Despite the assertions from the locals, very little changes tactically from state to state, and her new staff knew this well. She needed a smart, savvy campaign manager, and Jeff Angers fit the bill. And as always, the focus of critics' attention would be on her record, not her campaign manager's past.

Prochoice groups continued to rally against Pullen whenever they could. In January of 1992 with three months to go until the primary election, the local NOW chapter put out a call-to-action for a protest outside Pullen's state office on the anniversary of *Roe v. Wade*. They wanted to remind her that they were paying attention as she continued proposing more restrictions on abortion in the Illinois House. "Prochoice, my choice!" they shouted, armed with picket signs and marching around in circles. Fortunately for Pullen, they chose a date when she was not in the office.

Despite the condemnation from critics of her strident views on abortion, Pullen did not waiver. She felt part of the reason the race was so close last time was because her campaign allowed Mulligan to define her as a radical. She became controversial, and voters don't want a controversial person representing them in Springfield. She decided the best way to address the issue this time was to face it head on. She would not try to dodge the conversation or police her language when discussing abortion, she'd just state her views.

With a new campaign manager and campaign consultant came new tactics as well. Angers was looking for a way to cut through the noise and make sure voters knew who the real Penny Pullen was. The campaign put together a VHS tape entitled "The Penny Pullen Story." It was a new medium for electoral politics and made them stand out from the mountains of mail voters were receiving. The twelve-minute tape outlined Pullen's key accomplishments in the Illinois House including her four-year fight to repeal the inheritance tax. It addressed the issue of abortion unmistakably, making it clear that she was prolife and opposed to allowing minors to get an abortion without parental consent. Pullen made the case as to why the current abortion laws on the books in Illinois were too radical and needed to be changed. To close the presentation, she displayed a letter from a group of Democrats in the last election that was sent in support of her opponent. This was proof Mulligan was not a real Republican, she asserted. Not to mention, she lived outside the district. When the tape was finished, it was distributed to 1,000 undecided Republican voters throughout the district.

The videotape was all part of an effort to put forth positive messaging, something both campaigns insisted they were doing. By supposedly staying positive, the Pullen team hoped to set up a contrast between her and her opponent. On this point, Mulligan did not agree. "If you look at her campaign literature it's all very negative. It's always that the boogey man is going to get you if you don't do this . . . something terrible will happen to you," Mulligan said when asked about her opponent's advertising.[12]

Aside from new tactics and a new map, there was another factor that made this race different. Mike O'Malley, a thirty-five-year-old former Midway Airlines executive and accountant, decided to throw his hat in the ring as well. O'Malley had been involved locally as a Republican precinct captain in Des Plaines and even supported Pullen in 1990. At the time, if you wanted to be involved as a Republican precinct captain, there was no question you would support the incumbent. Backing the person in power was simply smart politics. Aside from his local involvement with the GOP, O'Malley was mostly unknown. Still, with a name like Mike O'Malley, he was sure to siphon off some votes. Primary day was set for March 17—Saint

Patrick's Day—and having an Irish last name certainly didn't hurt his candidacy. Mulligan took note of this, and was certain O'Malley was a plant who was sent for the sole purpose of weakening her.

There is a long mythology in the Chicagoland area of ethnic last names—particularly Irish names—being a boon to political candidates. This is especially true for races down ballot. Conventional wisdom says that an Irish surname is worth a few points electorally. It's nearly impossible to test the hypothesis, but it's based on the presumption that a good enough chunk of voters is simply too lazy to research who is on their ballot, so they just choose whoever sounds the most Irish.

Years later there would be a test case for this phenomenon. Phillip Spiwak was a criminal defense and bankruptcy attorney in suburban Chicago who decided to run for a seat on the Circuit Court of Cook County. It was a coveted post, often reserved for friends of the political machine. Spiwak was Polish, though, and his last name reflected that heritage. When he made his inaugural run, he lost the seat.

Spiwak thought hard about the strategy and any missteps his campaign may have made. Perhaps he needed more yard signs on busy highways? Should he have done better in his interview with the Illinois Bar Association? Maybe his message hadn't resonated with voters? In the end, Spiwak decided on a much simpler strategy. Before filing to run again for the judgeship, he legally changed his name to Shannon P. O'Malley. O'Malley won the seat by a comfortable margin.[13]

The truth was that *Mike* O'Malley—who didn't need to change his name—mostly entered the race to prove a point. He didn't think he'd have a shot defeating either candidate, but wanted to focus the party on uniting behind one candidate. But having an O'Malley in addition to a Mulligan on the same ballot was likely to benefit Pullen.

In late February, the Republican Women of Park Ridge held a candidate forum for the local races. Each candidate would have a few minutes to speak about their Republican credentials and why they should receive the support of the sixty-year-old GOP organization's members. The group was a bastion of conservatives and was particularly friendly to Pullen. Despite their partiality, Mulligan knew it was important for her to appear. For decades, Republican women's groups nationwide were an important constituency and reliable crop of volunteers. At a time when many women were homemakers, those with grown children were more willing to lick envelopes, write letters, and get engaged with campaigns. Local parties took advantage of this known base, and the Republican Women of Park Ridge was a prime example of this partisan phenomenon.

The three candidates showed up to the community center where the event was held. Both Mulligan and Pullen's supporters came wearing campaign buttons and holding signs displaying their support for their candidates as they spoke. Pullen gave an overview of her record and her usual campaign speech, highlighting her fights on conservative issues and her national appointments to various commissions. She attacked Mulligan too, questioning her support from labor unions and what taking money from these groups might mean about her ability to control the state's fiscal mess. Some attendees hissed as she attacked her opponent, shaking their heads in dismay.

Mulligan responded by holding up for the crowd a mailer that Pullen had sent out to voters. Pullen had pledged to run a positive campaign, she argued, but she's instead decided to appeal to "the worst side of human nature."[14] Again, jeers greeted Mulligan's assertions. The whole event made for a compelling scene in political theater.

In the end, the Republican Women of Park Ridge decided to hold off on an endorsement. For a group that had staunchly backed their hometown leader for decades, this was a huge loss for Pullen. She was failing to garner support from some of the people who previously backed her without question. No longer could she simply dismiss her opponent as a political dilettante.

The next joint appearance by the candidates came before another important Republican group, the Maine Township GOP. Maine Township comprised most of Park Ridge and Des Plaines, which covered nearly the entire district. Pullen was involved intimately with the local party ever since deciding to run for her boss's seat back in 1976. Just last election cycle, the group unanimously backed Pullen without so much as entertaining support for Mulligan. This time, however, would require much more persuasion. The previous GOP committeeman who was supportive of Pullen had been ousted in a bitter election fight and many of the local precinct captains—the ones who would ultimately vote on the endorsement—had been replaced in the past two years.

Serving as an elected GOP or Democratic committeeman whether on the county or state level is often a thankless position. If done right, you have a great amount of responsibility and power. At the same time, people blame you for everything that goes wrong both nationally and locally. As a cheerleader for the team, you bear the stench of anything the party does, no matter your involvement. Not to mention, the positions are almost always unpaid.

The three candidates again gathered at the Maine Township Hall. After the three were introduced to the packed room, Mike O'Malley began with a speech railing against both sides for their conduct. "I can no longer sit back and watch you fight with Rosemary," he said, staring squarely at Pullen. "You don't represent constituencies in your district," he continued. "You and Rosemary use the district for your own agenda." Many of the attacks echoed criticisms that had been leveled by the Mulligan campaign, and he even accused her of "Penny-mandering" the district to cut Mulligan out.[15] Despite his passion, O'Malley remained mostly a nonfactor in the race. He had raised only $5,000 and sent out a single mailer. Still, his attacks resonated with many of the people in the room. His point was to concentrate on electing Republicans and getting things done, not internal squabbling.

Unfazed by the attacks, Pullen approached the mic and began to speak. She reminded the more than 200 precinct captains of her fifteen-year record of accomplishments. She was protecting the public against AIDS, leading the fight on protecting unborn life, and concentrating on fixing local issues like the flooding problem that had long plagued the area. After about five minutes, she asked the crowd for their support and thanked them for the opportunity to address them.

As Pullen retreated from the microphone, Mulligan approached. She spoke about her usual issues of taxes, education, and crime. "It's the voters who are important to me," she said, echoing the criticism that Pullen was out of touch with her constituents.[16]

A simple majority of votes were required for an endorsement according to the organization's bylaws. With just 16 votes, Penny Pullen came in third place. O'Malley garnered 20 votes and 23 were cast for Mulligan. None of the three left the room with majority support from the most important Republican organization in the district. But Pullen needed the endorsement the most, and a failure to secure support was a clear sign that she was falling out of favor with local leaders. For Mulligan, Pullen's third-place finish was the cherry on top, and she clapped excitedly when it was announced no endorsement would be given.

One of the principal tasks of any local Republican organization like the Maine Township GOP is sending out a sample ballot in the mail to voters. This ballot highlights the endorsements of the organization and encourages the party loyalists to cast their vote for the endorsed slate. If the party didn't endorse in a particular race, they typically listed the candidates but indicated there was no endorsement. But this time around, the race was simply too contentious, and instead the organization decided to leave the 55th District entirely off the sample ballot.

To add insult to injury, the craziness of the campaign began to heat up again. At one point, a rock was thrown through the plate-glass windows of Pullen's office in Uptown Park Ridge. The incident caused Pullen to ask the police for extra patrols of her home and office to monitor any strange activity. This was the second time in three months something had been thrown at her office. "The cowards came in the middle of the night," said Joan Hall, one of her most prominent local supporters who served as her campaign chairwoman.[17] A constant presence at events and helping on the campaign trail, Hall proved invaluable to Pullen. She was full of charisma, and if you were walking around with the blonde-haired mother of two, you might easily confuse her for the town mayor by all the friends and acquaintances who greeted her.

Mulligan faced some chaos as well. She began receiving death threats and other harassing calls on her home phone from strangers. Her garage was egged on multiple occasions throughout the course of the campaign, and someone even drove over her lawn at night earlier that year, which her son reported to the police. When she went to a local parish to attend mass, she was told she couldn't receive communion and was eventually instructed not to come to church at all.[18] Rosemary Mulligan was no longer just a regular parishioner. She was the district's most well-known prochoice advocate, a twice-divorced candidate for state representative, and she was no longer welcome.

There was a tit for tat when it came to yard signs as well. In almost any campaign, it's not uncommon for supporters to steal signs or vandalize them with spray paint in local yards. In this race, many supporters took things to a whole new level. Some of the green Pullen signs were being set ablaze. "It was bad enough they were kicking and stealing our signs, but now they're putting lighter fluid or gasoline on them lighting them," Jeff Angers, Pullen's campaign manager, told a local paper just a few days before the March 17 primary.[19] It was a dramatic way of showing disdain for the candidate in an otherwise quiet suburban district. Other signs were being gathered up in the middle of the night from lawns and thrown in dumpsters around the district. Every little victory—no matter how petty—fueled the warring factions. The 1990 campaign had passionate supporters on both sides, but passion had turned to hatred by 1992.

• • •

Rosemary Mulligan at her polling place in Des Plaines and Penny Pullen in her polling place in Park Ridge on primary day—March 17, 1992. On each of their lapels is a shamrock, in honor of Saint Patrick's Day. Photo Credit: *Chicago Tribune*/TCA

13

Goldwater Girls

She's opened Pandora's box.

Students and faculty at Maine South High School crammed into a window-less classroom for a rare visit from a presidential candidate in March of 1992. Welcoming a high-profile political contender into its hallways was a first for the Park Ridge high school. Illinois rarely receives much political attention, but it just so happened that the presidential primary coincided with Penny Pullen and Rosemary Mulligan's election rematch set for March 17. Candidates for the 1992 Democratic nomination for president were also in the throes of a heated primary contest making its way through the state. The star of this particular visit, however, wasn't the candidate himself but his wife. "We're going to do something a little unusual today," the candidate told the crowd. "I came here to introduce my wife." Painted on long white butcher paper hanging from the wood-paneled walls was a message for the first lady of Arkansas: "Welcome Home Hillary!"

Maine South High School, built to keep up with the exploding population of the baby boom, counted in its first graduating class of 1965 a young Hillary Rodham among its ranks. Since then, many things had changed—including Hillary Rodham Clinton's politics. The Clintons were battling for the *Democratic* nomination, something her high school contemporaries probably wouldn't have foreseen.

"I know I should answer the question that is on very many of your minds—and that is—how did a nice Republican girl from Park Ridge go wrong?" she said to laughter. Standing atop a makeshift stage, Clinton took the audience through her political conversion. She and Governor Clinton then answered questions from the audience of eager students on the pressing issues of the day. Throughout, Clinton pointed to her education at Maine South as a catalyst for the change in her thinking about the world. As she paced back and forth with her husband seated on the stage behind her, Clinton wove in anecdotes about old teachers and former classmates with whom she had walked the halls.[1]

Park Ridge had been a Republican stronghold in the state for many decades, and most of the Rodham family, particularly Hillary Clinton's father, were staunch Republicans. As a high school student, she was active in her local Republican organization as a youth volunteer—a "Goldwater Girl"—supporting Arizona senator Barry Goldwater's run for president in 1964. Goldwater lost the election by a resounding margin against Lyndon Johnson, but his campaign was an inspiration to many modern conservatives.

While Clinton had experienced a political transformation, the same could not be said of all her old high school classmates. Indeed, Penny Pullen and Clinton were both members of the class of 1965, and Pullen had changed her views very little since then. Pullen had also worked as a Goldwater Girl, but the similarities mostly ended there. "She was part of the popular crowd, and I was not," Pullen recounted about her old classmate.[2] Clinton was involved in activities like student government while Pullen preferred keeping to the quieter corner of the high school's radio station.

Pullen remained a steady conservative even as a university student. At a time when boisterous anti—Vietnam War protests were making waves on campuses across the country, she steered away from the popular politics of her peers. Years later, Pullen would argue that many of her contemporaries would undergo a shift to the right and shun their youthful views. "They got out into the real world, got a job, became property owners and became more conservative," she remarked assuredly.[3] The same could not be said for Clinton, and Pullen attributed her old schoolmate's political leanings to her losing touch with her roots. "When Hillary left Park Ridge for Wellesley College, she was still a conservative Park Ridge girl," Pullen observed.[4]

The two women shared a mentor in high school in addition to their political proclivities. Paul Carlson was a popular history teacher who challenged them to think critically about politics and, in private conversations, tried to push them rightward. He was a self-described William F. Buckley conservative, and he counseled a host of impressionable students over the years. But while Pullen took Carlson's political advice to heart, Clinton began her leftward sway. Pullen thought the elite institution where Clinton went to college, coupled with the persuasion of her past youth minister, sowed the seeds for her political conversion. The two men were "locked in a battle for my mind and soul," Clinton would later recount.[5]

The first time Pullen saw Clinton after high school, she was shocked. Pullen was at her parents' home during college and turned on the *Irv Kupcinet Show*, a program hosted by the well-known *Chicago Sun-Times* columnist and sometimes fill-in at *The Tonight Show*. "She looked like a hippy with big glasses, shapeless clothes, and hair that looked like it hadn't been washed in a month," Pullen asserted. Clinton spoke about the issue of student housing at Wellesley, and Pullen quickly realized they no longer shared similar political leanings. The old Hillary Rodham—erstwhile Goldwater Girl—was no more.

Hillary Clinton was a high achiever in high school, but Pullen found her classmate to be calculating. She first saw this when it was time for their senior class at Maine South to vote on the annual Daughters of the American Revolution "Good Citizen Award." The award was given annually to the classmate who best embodied the qualities of dependability, service, leadership, and patriotism. The winner would then be granted a medal, some scholarship money, and coverage of the achievement in the local papers.

"I'm going after the DAR award," Clinton allegedly told Pullen. "It'll look good on my resumé," she said. Pullen thought it was inappropriate. "You got the award because of your concern for your country, not so you could get the award," she said when later recounting the scene.[6] Whether Pullen's concern was a genuine worry over the integrity of the process or merely a manifestation of her own jealousy is uncertain. Either way, her fellow classmates clearly did not share the same feelings and Clinton was bestowed the Good Citizen Award by her peers.

The two graduates of the class of 1965 hadn't spoken since leaving high school, but the political fate of both Penny Pullen and the Clintons would be up to Illinois voters in the Republican and Democratic primaries on Saint Patrick's Day 1992. On the Democratic side, voters would decide whether to allow the Clintons to continue their winning streak nationwide. For Republicans, incumbent President George H. W. Bush was the prohibitive favorite.

When Pullen opened her newspaper just a week before Election Day, she was shocked to see an advertisement featuring Mulligan with First Lady Barbara Bush. "She's one of us," it said in large text with the two shaking hands. Had the first lady issued an endorsement? It couldn't be true, her team thought.

The Pullen team called up some contacts at the White House to verify and faxed them a copy of the advertisement. The Bush team responded in due time, indicating that the first lady "had not endorsed any candidates in the race."[7] With just a few days left before Election Day, there was almost no time to correct the record.

• • •

Mulligan's team was quite pleased with the Barbara Bush ad. The idea came about when it was announced the first lady would be in town for a GOP fundraiser for the president's reelection campaign. Barbara Bush's approval rating was particularly high with Republican women, a demographic that both candidates needed to win over in order to earn the nomination. Armed with a $1,000 check, Mulligan went to the event, shook hands with the first lady, and came back with a photo fit for a new ad. The Pullen team insisted they issue an apology for the misleading photo, but Mulligan's team pushed back. After all, it didn't say *who* said "she's one of us." Perhaps that was Mulligan, making it known to the voters that she admired the first lady's politics. *Barbara Bush* is one of us.

The Mulligan team also prepared a mailer about her local roots and history growing up in the area. The hometown-themed piece displayed pictures of Mulligan in sepia tone. It depicted her as a little girl and her early life rooted in community. It had her family, all of whom were residents of the district and involved locally. And finally, it displayed a picture of her mother. The team was proud of the mailer, because they thought it showed the softer side of the candidate in an overheated race.

The 1992 campaign ran more smoothly for the Mulligan team, and she grew comfortable with letting others make decisions on things like mailers without her approval. She rarely critiqued the mail pieces and thought the firm they hired and those who wrote the copy did a wonderful job. The team was proud of this piece, though, so they decided to show it to Mulligan before it went out to voters. Mulligan looked at the draft and paused. "That's not my mom," she said.[8] After a few nervous laughs and sighs of relief, the mailer was edited to display her actual mother. They were all comfortable with one another after two campaigns, but there still wasn't room for error.

Having now run for office nearly nonstop for two years, Mulligan and her platform were well known to the editorial boards of all the local papers. During campaigns, candidates trek to the offices of news publications to answer questions from the people who cover them daily. Some papers hold editorial board sessions where both candidates attend, and the publication then decides on an endorsement. The encounters can often be contentious, with opposing candidates placed at separate ends of a long conference table and pitted against one another. Questioning then begins, and each person is peppered with difficult hypotheticals from ornery journalists and big-headed columnists from whom candidates would otherwise be shielded on the controlled environment of the campaign trail.

Mulligan had met all the players both in Chicago media and in the district, so the team was delighted when the *Chicago Tribune, Chicago Sun-Times*, and nearly all the local papers came through with full-throated endorsements. Their message was clear: it's time for someone new. Pullen retained the lone endorsement of the *Park Ridge Herald*. It was a relief for Pullen given that her first job out of college had been covering school board and township meetings as a part-time reporter for the weekly paper. In today's era of siloed political coverage and algorithm-driven social media, newspaper endorsements don't carry the weight they used to. But in 1992, a groundswell of support among the press was a huge boon to the Mulligan campaign.

As Election Day draws closer, campaigns enter a phase where accusations grow more frequent as rivals feel they're backed into a corner. It's silly season, a time to throw everything at the wall and see what sticks. "When a foe is cornered, they must fight for their lives and will do so with the energy of final fear," the famed Chinese general and philosopher Sun Tzu wrote in the 5th century B.C. in *The Art of War*. Tzu's words are often quoted by campaign junkies who have memorized a line or two despite never reading the whole book. It's an easy way to look smart. And on occasion, a connection between this ancient text's wise maxims can be drawn that isn't totally ludicrous in a contemporary political setting.

Near the end of February 1992, with just weeks to go before the March 17 primary, a surprise press conference was announced to the media in Chicago. The event was to be led by Tom Roeser, a conservative columnist, frequent guest on local television political programming, and former executive at Quaker Oats. A jowly man who spoke calmy and with poise, Roeser was adept at gaining the media's attention. With much suspense, Roeser announced to the press that he had filed a complaint against Rosemary Mulligan before the State Board of Elections for failing to disclose contributions from politically active law firms as well as a $5,000 check from a gay rights group. It was a shrewd and strategic way of forcing Mulligan to answer not just for alleged mismanagement of her campaign, but her willingness to take money from a group Roeser knew would cause her trouble in a GOP primary. Penny Pullen was nowhere to be found at the press conference, but there wasn't a shred of doubt in Mulligan's mind that her fingerprints were all over it, like a puppet master pulling the strings from afar. When asked for comment after the event, Pullen echoed many of the attacks made by Roeser and called law firms "clearinghouses of special interests."

"She's opened a Pandora's box," Mulligan responded. "This is clearly a pathetic attempt by a career politician to divert attention from any discussion of her record," she said, employing the dirtiest phrase an elected leader can be called.[9] There's nothing worse than a "career politician" in the eyes of the voters. It's a frequently used attack that also comes loaded with irony given those who use it often end up becoming career politicians themselves. Either way, Mulligan's team was furious. They felt confident any penalties would be thrown out, but answering the accusations would take time and energy from the campaign.

A hearing was scheduled by the Board of Elections to examine if the claims were justified. Barbara Scharringhausen, Mulligan's volunteer treasurer, would have to prepare to refute the accusations and ensure she had filed everything correctly. The position of treasurer is usually an unrewarded job. It requires organizing the often chaotic mess that is political fundraising. The person must keep track of all the receipts and incoming contributions, ensuring the campaign follows all regulations and reports things properly. And if she doesn't, her mistakes might cost the campaign a fine or potentially worse. The complaint *would* eventually be dismissed. And while Roeser had failed to get the campaign in trouble, he succeeded in wasting their time. Even small victories like these can make a difference in the waning days of a campaign.

Like a boomerang rushing back to its thrower, an ethics accusation also soon hit Pullen. For years, she advocated for abstinence education and opposed those who wanted to teach more comprehensive sex ed in schools. Pullen sat on the board of a group called the Committee on the Status of Women, which ran an abstinence education campaign called "Project Respect." In the legislature, Pullen had sponsored legislation requiring schools to teach abstinence education in any sex ed course. So when the group received $700,000 in state contracts, her political opponents pounced on the opportunity. One of her Democratic colleagues in the legislature held a press conference outside the State of Illinois Center in downtown Chicago and accused her of violating state ethics laws. There was a conflict of interest, he alleged, with Pullen sitting on the board of a group receiving state monies. "She's always talking about how much she saves our tax dollars by not voting for programs for education and senior citizens, then she votes to spend the taxpayer's money on something for her friends," Mulligan added to the fray, piggybacking on the attacks.[10]

"Pullen Accused of Ethics Violation," read one March headline.[11] With just two weeks to go before the March 17 primary, there was again little time to correct the record. While Pullen sat on the board of the group, she hadn't received any compensation and wouldn't benefit financially from any money the Committee on the Status of Women received. "Our young people are bombarded through MTV, popular music, and other cultural influences with messages that aggressively promote sexual promiscuity," she said in defense of the group. "My services with this organization is voluntarily given and it fits perfectly with my own political philosophy and the values of the constituents in my legislative district."[12]

· · ·

March 17, 1990, was the culmination of months of work. Rising before the sun, dozens of volunteers from both sides crisscrossed the district in the dark with temperatures just a few degrees above freezing. One at a time, volunteers would get out of their running car and force yard signs into the cold, hard ground at polling places across the 55th. Armed with a list of assignments, they would open the door to their car, run to the designated signage spot at each school, church, or rec center, then quickly retrace their steps back to the vehicle, taking a moment to warm up again and rev the engine toward the next location. On election morning, the sun peeked over the horizon at precisely 5:59 a.m. with just a minute to spare before the polls officially opened.

At each location, poll watchers for the teams arrived early for their shifts and volunteers for the campaigns staked out places in front of each entrance. They bundled up for the long haul, prepared for the chance of light rain during the day. For nearly two years, the district had been inundated with all things Pullen and Mulligan. Now came the moment of truth.

When the early morning tasks finished up, Mulligan and her most trusted confidants followed their tradition from the previous year and met for breakfast at a local diner. It was partly a celebration of their hard work and partly a way to distract Rosemary Mulligan from all the chaos swirling around her.

In the final weeks of a campaign, there is no more identifying potential voters. All the supporters have been located, and the final mission is ensuring they turn out to the polls. The Mulligan office was packed with people willing to help, and as the callers cycled through their lists, they crossed off voters who had already voted one by one. The ask is a simple question: *Have you voted yet?* Like a made-for-TV fundraising telethon, the office hummed with the unintelligible murmur of dozens of overlapping conversations. Campaign staffers scurried back and forth around the headquarters running on fumes. Volunteers raced through the front door and picked up their haul of literature before being swept out in a hurry to their assigned polling place. Like a beehive, the workers buzzed about, focused intently on the task at hand. The queen bee, meanwhile, had left to cast her vote.

Wearing a black winter coat with a green paisley scarf wrapped around her neck, Rosemary Mulligan entered her polling place and was greeted by the flash of cameras from local reporters. On her lapel sat a shamrock pin, a subtle reminder that today was Saint Patrick's Day.[13] Mulligan grabbed her ballot and approached the voting booth. While inside, Mulligan took a deep breath. Gripping the stylus, she worked her way down the ballot punching a hole firmly for each selection. When she finished, Mulligan rubbed her finger over her ballot to make sure no hanging chads remained.[14] She had learned the hard way that every vote matters, and she wasn't taking any chances.

The Mulligan team decided to hold their election night party in the office as they had the previous year. Spending money on a catered buffet wasn't an option either, so volunteers prepared "Mulligan stew" and brought their crockpots from home, a fitting dish for a Saint Patrick's Day election. Throughout the office, balloons floated to the ceiling and refreshments were scattered about. One voter remarked that it was time to drive the snakes, once and for all, out of the 55th District, a sentiment that Mulligan and her campaign staff shared, a reference to legend about Saint Patrick.

When the polls closed at 7 p.m., poll watchers and other volunteers came pouring into the office with their tapes from the precincts. Others grabbed the nearest phone to report the results back to headquarters. In a back room of the office away from the crowd, Mulligan's son Matt kept track of the incoming numbers. Things were looking up, and the crowd began to grow as the night went on. TV crews started entering the party as some began to think victory was afoot. "Ding dong, the wicked witch is dead!" a few ill-mannered supporters sang in anticipation.[15] They were quickly quieted down by others gathered in the office. The campaign team wanted to show that any victory was about a Mulligan victory, not a Pullen defeat.

The concession call is a time-honored tradition that first took place on the presidential level in 1968. An unofficial ritual in American politics, it's an exercise in humility. Running for office requires somewhat of an ego. Wallflowers need not apply. But upon defeat, once-boastful candidates must set aside their pride and signal to supporters that the battle is over. By 10 p.m. the results became clear, and ten minutes later, Penny Pullen called Rosemary Mulligan to concede the race.

Hearing the news, cheers began to break out in the office. Supporters hugged one another and toasted the victory. After two years of continuous campaigning, the race was finished. Mulligan was elated, hugging her son and bouncing around to supporters.

The local ABC 7 Chicago affiliate went live from the office for the ten o'clock news. "What's happening here is euphoria!" the reporter noted to cheers. "According to this campaign here at campaign headquarters they have said they have a report of 90 percent in and, Rosemary, you are declaring yourself the winner at this point?" "Well, I'm not but my campaign supporters are!" Mulligan said, laughing as her volunteers grinned and applauded.[16] Behind Mulligan, the office was packed shoulder to shoulder with people wearing green and pushing their way into the camera shot. Above her head hung a banner hung declaring "Pullen Dumped from Slate!" The room got quiet as the interview continued. "Were you expecting a close race once again?" she was asked. "I don't think if I ever continue this as my life's work I'll ever expect anything but a close race after what happened last time," Mulligan replied.[17]

As the celebration continued, calls poured in and Mulligan kept interviewing with reporters. Carol Moseley Braun became the Democratic nominee for U.S. Senate that night by defeating incumbent Senator Alan Dixon. As an incumbent, Dixon was the early favorite in the Democratic primary but Braun, a former state legislator and county official, used his support for Clarence Thomas's nomination to the Supreme Court as one of her principal attacks. Her victory was a milestone, as it would eventually make her the first Black woman elected to the United States Senate. But even while celebrating her victory, the soon-to-be Senator Moseley Braun called Mulligan to congratulate her on the win.

A call also came in from Minority Leader Lee Daniels. Daniels had been an ardent supporter of Pullen for years, having appointed her to leadership multiple times. He held fundraisers for her campaign, provided support during the recount fight, and was personal friends with Pullen too. Terry Cosgrove picked up the phone. "Hello, Citizens for Rosemary Mulligan," he answered with the sound of an excited crowd still registering the news in the background. He recognized the voice on the other end of the line. "Yes, this is Minority Leader Lee Daniels calling for Ms. Mulligan." Cosgrove wasted no time. "Lee, it's Terry Cosgrove. She's too busy to speak to you right now. I'll give her a message," he said, proceeding to hang up the phone.

Terry then approached Mulligan who was busy mingling with volunteers and thanking people for their support. He whispered into her ear that the Republican minority leader had just called to speak with her. "Well," she said. "I'll get back to him whenever I feel like it."[18]

• • •

Pullen's team had become regulars at the Chateau Rand, a banquet hall in Des Plaines. Over the years, conservative VIPs had flown into the district to shower praise upon Pullen during fundraising brunches and to support her reelection campaigns. But tonight was different, and the mood inside the banquet hall was somber.

Pullen was down by over a thousand votes, and it became clear the victory this time by Mulligan would be a decisive one. O'Malley had garnered little attention in the race, receiving just 7 percent of the vote. Penny Pullen had been a central target of prochoice activists for years, and they had finally succeeded at unseating their number-one target in Illinois.

Emerging from a back room where she and her team were monitoring results, Pullen announced the outcome to her gathered supporters. "The bad news is we didn't make it this time," she said with a subdued face. "The good news is, we won't have a recount." The room was stunned. They felt the attacks against Pullen had been dishonest and distorted. "The hug line starts here!"[19] she said with open arms and keeping a calm face. One by one, Pullen's most loyal supporters came to hug her and express their regret. Pullen's parents, always helpful throughout her campaigns, were there among the crowd and eminently proud of their daughter. Not far away were Pullen's twin sister and beloved niece who had recently moved back to the area and volunteered their time toward the effort. In some ways a defeat can feel like a funeral, and these supporters were mourning the death of a long career.

Pullen shared her supporters' disdain for the campaign that was run against her, but she also felt redeemed by running on her record and not shying away from her views on abortion. "When a political movement builds its base on lies, it can prevail for a season but only for a season," she told a reporter covering the party.

Many candidates would want to be left alone after a heart-wrenching defeat, but Penny Pullen faced the cameras for the local news with her faithful followers flanking her. Viewers' eyes were drawn immediately to her distinct red hair, which stood out against the dark background of the ballroom. She was stoic, with flushed cheeks and a look that betrayed the gravity of what had just happened. As always, there was a symbol of her politics on her jacket—a red rose, long an ode to the prolife movement.

The reporter put the microphone to Pullen's face and pressed her about the outcome. "The people of the 55th District appear indeed to have spoken, and to have chosen their next representative for the next two years," she said, conceding defeat. Pullen finished with a note about how she felt the campaign had gone. "We have the satisfaction of knowing that we did not swerve on principle and we did not do anything in this campaign we could be ashamed of, and so we can walk away with our heads held high," she continued, with bright lights shining on her face. As the reporter then faced the camera and turned viewers back to the anchor's desk in Chicago, Pullen's supporters erupted in cheers. It was a final celebration, a last chance to applaud their fearless leader. As people clapped around her in approval, Pullen managed to keep a smile.[20]

Discussion that night quickly turned to an autopsy of the race. Should she have taken the challenge more seriously the first time around? Where would she be if the abortion issue had been addressed out front? Was she simply just too conservative for the district? Still, she was clearly in defeat. A letter was drafted later to send out to supporters. "Yes, we lost the election Tuesday. Rosemary Mulligan is the Republican nominee from the 55th Representative District of Illinois."[21]

Just as Pullen said, there would be no recount this time. The result was clear and the voters of the 55th District had spoken. After she finished greeting her supporters and receiving their condolences, Pullen went home and went to bed. The final tally was 5,434 votes for Pullen to Mulligan's 6,638.[22]

As the sun rose on the district the next morning, the yard signs that covered front lawns across the area were illuminated once again. Just hours earlier, there had been a mad dash to cover the district with the candidate's names and make it known that Election Day had arrived. For Pullen, the signs were now useless, artifacts of a period in her life that was now coming to a close.

There are few things as ephemeral as a political campaign. The intensity rises slowly, hitting its peak at the very end. Then all of the sudden, it comes to a haunting close. Any outstanding items on the to-do list are no longer to be done. There are no fundraisers to be attended. No doors to be knocked. No voters to be called.

The campaign was over. The votes had been cast. And the voters who each candidate had long courted with an exhausting intensity went back to their everyday lives.

Epilogue

A motorcade of black SUVs pulled up outside a nondescript, two-story office building off busy Lee Street in suburban Des Plaines, Illinois, on October 26, 2007. As the cars rolled to a stop, a state trooper rushed around the vehicle to open the door as Governor Rod Blagojevich put his feet to the ground and began walking toward the entrance. Although he was elected by comfortable margins, the governor's popularity had taken a nosedive following his 2006 reelection after a series of missteps and impending federal investigations that threatened to totally derail his administration. Sensing no support for his agenda from members of his Democratic party, Blagojevich found himself turning to Republicans to see if they could find common cause. Armed with his signature well-coifed black hair and standard pricey custom-tailored suit, the governor had requested a meeting with State Representative Rosemary Mulligan, by then a longtime Republican legislator.

Mulligan greeted the state's chief executive at the door as they entered the office complex with bystanders pausing to observe the hullabaloo and snap pictures. Having been a legislator for years, Mulligan made it a habit to always bring a staff member or a trusted advisor to important meetings like these so there would be no second-guessing what happened. As the governor and his staffer got settled into Mulligan's office, they exchanged pleasantries about the weather and other innocuous issues. Eventually, Mulligan was ready to dispense with the niceties and begin the meeting. "Well, governor, I suppose you want to know why I don't like you," she said bluntly. A brief moment of silence ensued as Blagojevich and his aide looked at one another. Mulligan continued her thought. "You got a mandate with your vote to do wonderful, bright things for the people of Illinois and you've blown it," she said, never mincing words.[1] What was planned as a twenty-minute meeting turned into a two-hour session. The governor pushed hard for Mulligan to go along with some of his legislative items, but she was unmoved. His agenda wasn't her agenda, but she appreciated the gesture nonetheless. Most legislators thought he was a crook, but Mulligan respected the office he held enough to sit down with him. Still, she was unfazed. "He'll be arrested within a year," she quipped to her former aide who had joined the meeting.[2]

After defeating Penny Pullen in the 1992 Republican primary, Rosemary Mulligan went on to handily beat her Democratic opponent in the general election and was then sworn in the following January to the Illinois State House. She served for twenty years, from 1993 to 2013. Over time, she became known as someone who always spoke her mind, sometimes to a fault. Years later, she'd be caught on a hot mic on the Illinois House floor calling Blagojevich a "blithering idiot," a remark that caused some momentary commotion in the Chicago press.[3] Whenever Mulligan felt a witness wasn't being honest with her during committee hearings, she wouldn't hold back. "You know what, there's a lot of us that are fed up with the bullshit!" she yelled from her perch on the dais to one witness she thought was obfuscating. "Oh, I don't think that was necessary, representative," the witness replied. "I think it's *very* necessary!" she quipped, never one to apologize for injecting some passion into a subject she cared about deeply.[4] When quoted in the local papers in her district, Rosemary Mulligan was often so brutally honest that a casual reader might be convinced she was unaware she would be quoted.

During her time in the legislature, Rosemary Mulligan focused on a variety of issues, but particularly concentrated on expanding human services to the elderly and indigent, tackling prescription drug prices, and working to address other healthcare issues. She became known as an expert on the state's healthcare budget, an item she studied intensely. Her colleagues in the state House often remarked how quickly she could pull obscure facts and figures from her head merely from memory. When Illinois legalized civil unions for same-sex couples in 2011, Mulligan cast one of the tie-breaking votes. As the HIV/AIDS virus continued to remain a pressing public health issue, she was instrumental in increasing state funding to care for those affected. Partly driven by her own experience dealing with her son's struggle with gambling, Mulligan introduced legislation to require lottery tickets and off-track betting facilities to display a help hotline for compulsive gamblers. For this work, she was honored by the National Council on Problem Gambling.

And of course, Rosemary Mulligan was a staunch prochoice advocate in the Illinois House during her tenure. She was an Illinois Republican. In many states, Mulligan might have been a Democrat. Rosemary Mulligan and Penny Pullen represent two sides of the Republican party that still quarrel today.

In her final term of office, seventy-one-year-old Rosemary Mulligan was forced into retirement after failing to make the ballot. The truth is, Mulligan was near the end of her career, and it was time to go. But it turns out her retirement was more of an instruction from Republican leadership than a voluntary decision. They wanted fresh blood in the seat, particularly because she sometimes bucked the party trend. It was partly Mulligan's fault for not being prepared and partly sabotage on the part of House Republican leadership. After twenty years, her time had passed for casting votes down in Springfield.

During the competition to replace her that year, Mulligan went on to endorse the Democrat in the race. Some local Republicans brushed it off as more proof that Mulligan really had been a Democrat all along. She attributed her decision to sharing the Democratic candidate's prochoice views and insisted the Republican was simply too conservative for the district. But little did some know that the endorsement had little to do with the current candidates and everything to do with her old rival Penny Pullen, who was supporting the Republican. After more than twenty years, the *Pullen v. Mulligan* battle was revived anew.

Two decades of shuttling back and forth between Springfield and her home in Des Plaines took a toll on Mulligan's health over time. The seat that she occupied was almost always under attack during her tenure, whether from Democratic House Speaker Mike Madigan or a primary challenge from the right. "You wake in the middle of the night with your stomach aching," she observed years later when describing the nonstop fear of being unseated. "I would never relax. I stay vigilant to the end."[5] Barely two years after leaving the state House, Rosemary Mulligan died in December of 2014 at age seventy-three.

• • •

Following the 1992 election, Penny Pullen continued working in politics in a variety of capacities. In 1992, she was named the first executive director of the Illinois Family Institute, a socially conservative advocacy group dedicated to issues like promoting prolife legislation, fighting against gay marriage, and supporting policies that benefit home schooling. Penny Pullen also created Life Advocacy Resource Project, a group that is devoted to coaching conservative candidates how to talk about abortion. In many ways, it's a reaction to her 1990 and 1992 campaigns where some blamed her eventual loss for trying to hide from her prolife views. Her lesson to candidates today is to address the issue head-on.

Pullen also remained active in state and local politics for years following her exit from the state House. She served as president of the Eagle Forum of Illinois, a national group founded by Phyllis Schlafly, and maintained involvement with national conservative organizations like the Council on National Policy, a cadre of conservative VIPs that gathers semiannually behind closed doors. During her early years in the legislature, she was one of the founding members of the American Legislative Exchange Council, a powerful organization that serves as a clearinghouse for conservative legislation on the state level. She is still active in her local Republican party and continues her lifelong prolife advocacy. Pullen is the type of person who works quietly behind the scenes without the need for praise or credit to keep herself motivated.

When socially conservative candidates were contemplating a run for office in Illinois, they would often turn to Pullen for advice. As presidential candidates were courting support in the Illinois primary in 2012, Pullen endorsed former Pennsylvania senator Rick Santorum, the person who most aligned closely with her self-described profamily views. Santorum came to Illinois to campaign in 2012 while facing off in a heated primary against Mitt Romney. Gathered before a crowd of thousands in suburban Arlington Heights, the surging candidate was introduced to a receptive audience in a packed high school gymnasium. Clapping on the stage of dignitaries just a few feet away from the presidential contender sat Penny Pullen. Twenty years after leaving office, her status as a conservative luminary in Illinois was still rock-solid. Today, she lives in Michigan with her twin sister, Pam Reed.

· · ·

This book tells the specific story of Pullen and Mulligan's fight in the 55th District of Illinois, a wild example of how state legislative politics can capture national attention. But the truth is, there are thousands of stories just like this one. Across the country, state and local elections make a difference on the lives of Americans each year. And even without national media attention, state and local races are exceedingly important.

Fewer than one in five Americans can even name their state legislator, but chances are they've felt the impact of something that person has voted on in their state capitol.[6] The average state legislator in a leadership position or committee chairmanship has more power and influence on our lives than a run-of-the-mill member of Congress. The difference? State leaders mostly fly under the radar. Americans need to understand that local politics—whether at the municipal, county, or state level—is arguably more consequential than the national political battles capturing our attention.

Whether you think obtaining a gun is too easy or believe the Second Amendment is under assault, your issue is decided down ballot. Whether you believe voting rights are being nefariously restricted or voter ID laws are paramount to securing our elections, your issue is decided down ballot. Whether you think religious freedom is being attacked or religion is invading the public sphere, your issue is decided down ballot. This story is proof that now more than ever, those concerned about the debate over abortion— or any fraught political issue—should be paying attention to state and local races. The point of this story was to evoke in each reader a simple question: Do you know what's happening down ballot?

Notes

Introduction

1. Vince Morris, "Boies Will Be Boies! He Loses Cool on TV," *New York Post*, December 11, 2000.

2. Abdon M. Pallasch, "Michael E. Lavelle Sr.: Dean of Chicago Election Lawyers—1938–2009," *Chicago Sun-Times*, December 23, 2009.

3. Karen Donovan, *v. Goliath: The Trials of David Boies* (New York: Vintage, 2007), 280–82, 287–89.

4. Jake Tapper, *Down & Dirty: The Plot to Steal the Presidency* (New York: Little, Brown, 2001), 244–50, 285–90, 364–65.

5. Morris, "Boies Will Be Boies!"

6. "State Legislatures vs. Congress: Which Is More Productive?" Quorum, https://www.quorum.us/data-driven-insights/state-legislatures-versus-congress-which-is-more-productive/.

Chapter 1. Amendment XXVII

1. Penny Pullen, interview by Mark DePue, session 1, April 15, 2020, Legislators Project, Abraham Lincoln Presidential Library and Museum, Springfield, IL.

2. Ibid.

3. Ibid.

4. Ibid.

5. Erin Blakemore, "Why the Fight of Over the Equal Rights Amendment Has Lasted Nearly a Century," *History.com*, March 21, 2022.

6. *Chicago Tonight,* episode no. 5034, aired August 27, 1987, on WTTW Chicago.

7. Lee Edwards, "How Phyllis Schlafly Beat Liberal GOP Kingmakers and Paved Way for Reagan," *Daily Signal*, September 6, 2016.

8. Taylor Pensoneau, "Shipley-Schlafly Race: Battle of Sexes," *St. Louis Post-Dispatch*, October 27, 1970.

9. Edward McClelland, "When Illinois Conservatives Blocked the ERA," *Chicago Magazine*, January 16, 2020.

10. Eileen Ogintz, "Anti-ERA Group Finds Other Issues," *Chicago Tribune*, October 23, 1979.

11. "Rep. Pullen Looks Up to God in Waging Anti-abortion Fight," *Bloomington Pantagraph*, October 19, 1989.

12. Lila Thulin, "Why the Equal Rights Amendment Is Still Not Part of the Constitution," *Smithsonian Magazine*, November 13, 2019.

13. Proposed Amendment to the Constitution of the United States, H. J. Res. 208, 92nd Cong., 2nd sess. (1971).

14. Mary Gillespie, "She Has a Righteous Perspective—Rep. Penny Pullen Listens to Her Heart," *Chicago Sun-Times*, August 12, 1987.

15. Ogintz, "Anti-ERA Group Finds Other Issues.

16. Ibid.

17. "People & Ideas: Jerry Falwell," "God in America," *Frontline* and *The American Experience*, aired October 2020, PBS, https://www.pbs.org/wgbh/pages /frontline/godinamerica/people/jerry-falwell.html.

18. "TV Preacher's Road Show Stages Anti-ERA Rally on Capitol Steps," *St. Louis Post-Dispatch,* May 7, 1980.

19. STOP ERA ad, *Chicago Tribune*, April 28, 1980, A3.

20. Anne Keegan, "A Fighting Lady's Down but Not Out," *Chicago Tribune*, August 26, 1980.

21. David Axelrod, "Public Support of ERA Dropping, Poll Finds," *Chicago Tribune*, May 20, 1980.

22. Susan Llork, "Letters: Women's Lib Has Made a Real Mess," *Chicago Sun-Times*, September 3, 1987.

23. Daily Diary of President Jimmy Carter, June 18, 1980, Jimmy Carter Presidential Library and Museum, Atlanta, GA.

24. Mitchell Locin and Daniel Egler, "ERA Rejected Again in House Showdown," *Chicago Tribune*, June 19, 1980.

25. Philip Lentz and Daniel Egler, "ERA Fast 'Like Being in Zoo,'" *Chicago Tribune*, May 30, 1982.

26. Ibid.

27. Ibid.

28. Mark DePue, "An Unlikely Defeat: The ERA Fight in Illinois," Illinois State Museum, January 8, 2020, https://www.illinoisstatemuseum.org/content/unlikely -defeat-era-fight-illinois.

29. Pullen, interview.

Chapter 2. Rosemary Mulligan

1. Steve Granzyk, interview with author, October 23, 2022.

2. "Come to Park Ridge and Live," Pieces of Park Ridge Collection, Illinois Digital Archives, http://www.idaillinois.org/digital/collection/parkridg003/id/206.

3. Amy Wooten, "Illinois State Rep. Rosemary Mulligan Faces Challenges," *Windy City Times*, September 10, 2008.

4. Steve Granzyk, interviews with author, August 1 and August 5, 2022.

5. History, Maine Township High School District 207, https://maine207.org /history/.

6. *Lens*, Maine Township High School yearbook, Graduating Class of 1958, 68, 169.

7. Matt Bonaguidi, interview with author, October 6, 2021.

8. Rosemary Mulligan, "Mulligan Tells Why She'll Run in 55th District," *Des Plaines Journal*, December 11, 1991.

9. Walter Gottesman, "Obituary: Ex-Des Plaines Ald. Daniel Bonaguidi," *Chicago Tribune*, July 20, 2000.

10. "Parents Tell of Engagements," *Chicago Daily Tribune*, October 20, 1960.

11. "Obituary: Daniel Robert Bonaguidi," Dignity Memorial, https://www .dignitymemorial.com/obituaries/des-plaines-il/daniel-bonaguidi-10048227.

12. Ted Saylor, "Mulligan No Stranger to Tragedy," *Des Plaines Journal*, November 13, 1991.

13. *People v. Hubbard*, 55 Ill. 2d 142, 146 (1973).

14. Granzyk, interviews, August 1 and August 5, 2022.

15. Saylor, "Mulligan No Stranger to Tragedy."

16. Ibid.

17. Sheila Peters, "Saturday, Sept. 18, 1982," *Sheila Peters Blog*, https://sheilapeters. com/tag/emil-mesich/.

18. "Crash of a De Havilland DHC-3 Otter in Leo Creek: 3 Killed," November 26, 1979, Bureau of Aircraft Accidents Archives, https://www.baaa-acro.com/city /leo-creek.

19. Ibid.

20. "Crash of Emil Mesich's Plane," September 1982, Joseph Alle L'Orsa Map and Photograph Collection, Bulkley Valley Museum, https://search.bvmuseum.org/link /descriptions6290.

21. Peters, "Saturday, Sept. 18, 1982."

22. Bonaguidi, interview.

23. "Obituary: Daniel Robert Bonaguidi."

24. Saylor, "Mulligan No Stranger to Tragedy."

Chapter 3. Blood Terrorists

1. Joseph Bennington-Castro, "How AIDS Remained an Unspoken—But Deadly— Epidemic for Years," *History.com*, June 1, 2020.

2. Executive Order 12601—Presidential Commission on the Human Immuno- deficiency Virus Epidemic, June 24, 1987, Ronald Reagan Presidential Library, Simi Valley, CA.

3. Mary Gillespie, "She Has a Righteous Perspective—Rep. Penny Listens to Her Heart," *Chicago Sun-Times*, August 12, 1987.

4. Kirk Kidwell, "Public Health Officials, Do Your Jobs!" *New America*, May 23, 1988.

5. Thomas Hardy, "Pullen a Backer of AIDS Testing," *Chicago Tribune*, July 24, 1987.

6. Bernard Turnock, correspondence with author, September 2, 2022.

7. Daniel Egler, "Repeal of AIDS Law Gains," *Chicago Tribune*, April 12, 1989.

8. Sandra Boodman, "Premarital AIDS Testing Annoying Many in Illinois; Some Couples Head Out of State to Say 'I Do,'" *Washington Post*, July 30, 1988.

9. John Kass and Steve Daley, "The AIDS Dilemma," *Chicago Tribune*, September 6, 1987.

10. Bob Secter, "Leave State to Avoid Required Step for Marriage License: Illinois Couples Shun AIDS Tests," *Los Angeles Times*, October 14, 1988.

11. Boodman, "Premarital AIDS Testing Annoying Many in Illinois."

12. Rick Pearson, "Thompson Weighs Future of AIDS Tests," *Chicago Tribune*, September 11, 1989.

13. Daniel Egler and Jack Houston, "Thompson Calls AIDS Rap 'Garbage,'" *Chicago Tribune*, April 22, 1987.

14. Ibid.

15. Gillespie, "She has a Righteous Perspective—Rep. Penny Listens to Her Heart."

16. Ibid.

17. Sandra Boodman, "AIDS Panel Appointed by Reagan; President Visits Ill Children at NIH," *Washington Post*, July 24, 1987.

18. Diane Bernard, "Three Decades before Coronavirus, Anthony Fauci Took Heat from AIDS Protesters," *Washington Post*, May 20, 2020.

19. President Reagan's Remarks at a Panel Discussion on AIDS Research at the National Institutes of Health (NIH), Bethesda, MD, July 23, 1987, Ronald Reagan Presidential Library.

20. *ABC World News Tonight*, aired July 23, 1987.

21. Sandra Boodman, "Views of 4 U.S. AIDS Panelists Hit," *Washington Post*, August 26, 1987.

22. Gillespie, "She has a Righteous Perspective—Rep. Penny Listens to Her Heart."

23. Sandra Boodman, "Protests Expected as AIDS Panel Meets," *Washington Post*, September 9, 1987.

24. Sandra Boodman, "Views of 4 U.S. AIDS Panelists Hit," *Washington Post*, August 26, 1987.

25. *ABC World News Tonight*, aired July 23, 1987.

26. Julie Johnson, "Washington Talk: The First Lady; Strong Opinions with No Apologies," *New York Times*, May 25, 1988.

27. Interim Draft Report on AIDS, C-SPAN, aired February 29, 1988, https://www.c-span.org/video/?1814–1/interim-draft-report-aids.

28. Kristine Gebbie, interview with author, September 15, 2021.

29. Tim Drake, interview with Tracy Baim, August 16, 2007, *Chicago Gay History*, "AIDS Personal Political Histoy" [sic], https://www.chicagogayhistory.com/video_bio.php?id=759.

30. Discussion of Final Report to President, C-SPAN, aired June 7, 1988, https://www.c-span.org/video/?28761/discussion-final-report-president.

31. Sandra Boodman, "AIDS Panel Recommends Law Banning Discrimination; Final Report to Be Sent to President by Friday," *Washington Post*, June 18, 1988.

32. William Lanouette, "James D. Watkins: Frustrated Admiral of Energy," *Bulletin of the Atomic Scientists*, January/February 1990.

33. Gebbie, interview.

34. Discussion of Final Report to President.

35. Sandra Boodman, "Commissions' Chief Faults AIDS Response," *Washington Post*, June 3, 1988.

36. Epigraph to *Report of the Presidential Commission on the Human Immuno-deficiency Virus Epidemic*, June 24, 1988, https://www.ojp.gov/pdffiles1/Digitization /112422NCJRS.pdf.

37. Sandra Boodman, "Reagan Accepts AIDS Panel Report; President Withholds Comment on Key Antibias Recommendation," *Washington Post*, June 28, 1988.

38. Boodman, "AIDS Panel Recommends Law Banning Discrimination."

Chapter 4. Henry Penny

1. Rob Karwath, "Pullen Leads Abortion Foes' Fight," *Chicago Tribune*, September 26, 1989.

2. Michael Hirsley, "Abortion Foes Press Lutheran Hospital," *Chicago Tribune*, August 19, 1989.

3. Hugo Kristensson, "Letter to the Editor: Pullen's Time as Legislator Is Past," *Park Ridge Advocate*, March 15, 1990.

4. Penny Pullen, interview by Mark DePue, session 2, April 22, 2020, Legislators Project, Abraham Lincoln Presidential Library and Museum, Springfield, IL.

5. Penny Pullen, interview by Mark DePue, session 3, April 29, 2020, Legislators Project, Abraham Lincoln Presidential Library and Museum, Springfield, IL.

6. Lynn Sweet, "Pullen, Primary Foe Play Down Abortion," *Chicago Sun-Times*, March 14, 1990.

7. Mary Gillespie, "She Has a Righteous Perspective—Rep. Penny Listens to Her Heart," *Chicago Sun-Times*, August 12, 1987.

8. Pullen, interview, session 3.

9. Robert Rakow Jr., "Pullen, Mucci Tackle Issues at Low-Key Political Debate," *Park Ridge Times Herald*, October 31, 1990.

10. 83rd Illinois General Assembly, House Transcript, May 27, 1983.

11. R. Bruce Dold, "Legislature's Heavy Hitters," *Chicago Tribune*, July 15, 1983.

12. Shirley Siluk, "Not All Pullen Awards Listed on Her Resume," *Park Ridge Advocate*, December 14, 1989.

13. "'Warrior' Pullen Steams On Despite Battles," *Daily Herald*, October 29, 1989.

14. Isaac Stanley-Becker, "Henry Hyde, Abortion Amendment's Namesake, Was a Culture Warrior with Some Surprising Causes," *Washington Post*, June 7, 2019.

15. Adam Clymer, "Former Rep. Henry Hyde Is Dead at 83," *New York Times*, November 30, 2007.

16. Sarah McCammon, "Biden's Budge Proposal Reverses a Decades-Long Ban on Abortion Funding," *NPR*, May 31, 2021.

17. *Webster v. Reproductive Health Services*, 492 U.S. 490 (1987).

18. Evan Thomas, "How the Supreme Court Justice Sandra Day O'Connor Helped Preserve Abortion Rights," *New Yorker*, March 27, 2019.

19. Jennifer Halperin, "House Panel Oks Abortion Curb Doctors to Decide If Fetus Can Survive," *Chicago Tribune*, April 14, 1987.

20. Jennifer Halperin, "House Panel Oks Abortion Curb," *Chicago Tribune*, April 4, 1989.

21. 86th Illinois General Assembly, House Transcript, June 24, 1989.

22. Lynn Sweet and Fran Spielman, "Fight Looms in Springfield—'The Hottest Session since ERA' Predicted," *Chicago Sun-Times*, July 4, 1989.

23. Kurt Greenbaum, "Bill to Safeguard the Unborn Raises a Storm of Questions," *Chicago Tribune*, May 11, 1986.

24. Pullen, interview, session 3.

25. Lou Cannon, "Reagan Pledges He Would Name a Woman to the Supreme Court," *Washington Post*, October 15, 1980.

26. Evan Thomas, *First* (New York: Random House, 2019), 92.

27. Office of the President, Tapes of Dictation: Records, 1981–1982, Reel #3—Documents 11A–11K, Ronald Reagan Presidential Library, Simi Valley, CA.

28. *Webster v. Reproductive Health Services*, 492 U.S. 490 (1987).

29. Robin Tober, "Abortion Marchers Gather in Capital," *New York Times*, April 9, 1989.

30. "State Abortion Battle Predicted," *Park Ridge Advocate*, July 6, 1989.

31. Robert Rakow Jr., "Pullen Praises Abortion Decision, Sees New Bans," *Park Ridge Times Herald*, July 5, 1989.

32. Terence E. Fretheim, "Pullen Comments 'Hitlerian,'" *Des Plaines Suburban Times*, July 12, 1989.

33. "State Abortion Battle Predicted," *Park Ridge Advocate*, July 6, 1989.

34. "Rep. Pullen Looks Up to God in Waging Anti-abortion Fight," *Bloomington Pantagraph*, October 19, 1989.

35. Dave Urbanek, "GOP Representative Won't Change Mind on Tough Pro-choice Stance," *Daily Herald*, October 19, 1989.

36. "Anti-abortionists Rally at Illinois Capitol," *Daily Herald* (UPI), October 19, 1989.

37. "Rep. Pullen Looks Up to God."

38. Urbanek, "GOP Representative Won't Change Mind."

39. "'Warrior' Pullen Steams On Despite Battles."

40. Rick Pearson, "Illinois Abortion Bill Blocked, Plan to Tighten Curbs 1 Vote Shy in House Committee," *Chicago Tribune*, October 18, 1989.

Chapter 5. Two Cents

1. "Death Notices: BARTOLINI," *Chicago Tribune*, June 19, 1989.

2. Shirley Siluk, "The Difference a Year Makes," *Park Ridge Advocate*, October 19, 1989.

3. Ibid.

4. "NOW Chapter Sets Pro-choice March," *Park Ridge Times Herald*, October 11, 1989.

5. Siluk, "The Difference a Year Makes."

6. Ibid.

7. Ibid.

8. Ibid.

9. Amy Wooten, "Illinois State Rep. Rosemary Mulligan Faces Challenges," *Windy City Times,* September 10, 2008.

10. Ibid.

11. Ellen Yearwood, interview with author, October 1, 2021.

Chapter 6. On the Trail

1. Geraldine Tarbutton, "Letters: Speak Out for Freedom of Choice," *Park Ridge Herald*, October 25, 1989.

2. "Talk of the Town: 'What Choice?'" *Park Ridge Times Herald*, November 8, 1989.

3. Carroll Salman, "Pro-choice Republican to Face Pullen in Primary," *Park Ridge Times Herald,* November 1, 1989.

4. Ibid.

5. Mary Ann Irvine, interview with author, September 1, 2021.

6. Ibid.

7. Diddy Blythe, interview with author, August 17, 2021.

8. Terry Cosgrove, interview with author, August 23, 2021.

9. Jeff Diamant, "Three-in-Ten or More Democrats and Republicans Don't Agree with Their Party on Abortion," *Pew Research Center*, June 18, 2020.

10. Terry Cosgrove, interview with Tracy Baim, May 9, 2007, *Chicago Gay History*, https://www.chicagogayhistory.com/video_bio.php?id=815.

11. Madeleine Doubek, "Abortion Tops Agenda in 55th District Race," *Daily Herald,* December 13, 1989.

12. Barbara Brotman, "Pullen Race Vital to Both Sides on Abortion," *Chicago Tribune*, February 18, 1990.

13. "Local Political Briefs," *Park Ridge Times Herald*, January 31, 1989.

14. Blythe, interview.

15. "Challengers Pick Up Steam in Hot Legislative Primaries," *Daily Herald*, March 12, 1990.

16. Shirley Siluk, "Pullen Won't Debate over Debate," *Park Ridge Advocate*, January 25, 1990.

17. Eddy McNeil, "Pullen Bucks Trend toward Democrats," *Chicago Tribune*, November 5, 1982.

18. "Letters: Pullen's Record Needs No Debate," *Park Ridge Advocate*, February 15, 1990.

19. Joshua Stewart and Lyndsay Winkley, "Lucy Killea, Independent Trailblazer, Mentor to Women, Dies," *San Diego Tribune*, January 18, 2017.

20. Cosgrove, interview with author.

Chapter 7. Raccoons, Reporters, and Rapists' Rights

1. John Giangrasse Kates, "Ralph A. Barger, 79," *Chicago Tribune*, April 5, 2022.

2. "Barger Takes Seat for 39th District," *Illinois Issues*, March 1983.

3. Katherine Seigenthaler, "Pullen Pulls Out Stops for Barger," *Chicago Tribune*, March 19, 1990.

4. Ibid.

5. Shirley Siluk, "Not All Pullen Awards Listed on Her Resume," *Park Ridge Advocate*, December 14, 1989.

6. Shirley Siluk, "55th GOP Voters Face First Primary in Decade," *Park Ridge Advocate*, March 8, 1990.

7. Anonymous source.

8. "Obituary: Rosemary Mulligan," Dignity Memorial, https://www.dignitymemorial.com/obituaries/des-plaines-il/rosemary-mulligan-6261568.

9. Laura Biachi, "The Takeaway—Terry Cosgrove," *Crain's Chicago Business*, October 30, 2017.

10. Margaret Sullivan, "Every Week, Two More Newspapers Close—and 'News Deserts' Grow Larger," *Washington Post*, June 29, 2022.

11. "Mulligan Attacks Pullen's Record on Children's Issues," *Park Times Ridge Herald*, February 21, 1990.

12. Fran Spielman and Jim Merriner, "Partee Rips Cop's Role in TV Ad for O'Connor," *Chicago Sun-Times*, March 15, 1990.

13. Mary Ann Irvine, interview with author, September 1, 2021.

14. *Chicago Tonight*, episode no. 5034, aired August 27, 1987, on WTTW Chicago.

15. Daniel Egler, "GOP Girding for Battle in Issue-Oriented Primary," *Chicago Tribune*, February 4, 1990.

16. Rob Secter, "Abortion Emerging as Year's No. 1 Issue in Many Local Elections across the U.S.," *Los Angeles Times*, March 18, 1990.

17. Ibid.

18. Ad, *Des Plaines Journal*, March 14, 1990.

19. Rob Karwath, "Pullen Leads Abortion Foes' Fight," *Chicago Tribune*, September 26, 1989.

20. Calvin L. Skinner Jr. Papers, Northern Illinois University Regional History Center, DeKalb, IL.

21. Ad, *Des Plaines Suburban Times,* March 7, 1990.

Chapter 8. GOTV

1. "Pullen-Mulligan Contest Was 'Rolling in Dough,'" *Des Plaines Journal*, August 8, 1990.

2. Terry Cosgrove, interview with author, August 23, 2021.

3. Vicki Speer, "Pullen's Patience Prevails," *Daily Herald*, September 30, 1990.

4. "Opinion: Mulligan's Brother Responds to Letter," *Park Ridge Advocate*, April 26, 1990.

5. Shirley Siluk, "Mulligan the Winner by 31," *Park Ridge Advocate*, March 22, 1990.

6. *ABC World News,* March 21, 1990.

7. Anonymous source.

Chapter 9. Dimpled Chads

1. Shirley Siluk, "Mulligan the Winner by 31," *Park Ridge Advocate*, March 22, 1990.

2. "Street Talk," *Park Ridge Times Herald*, March 28, 1990.

3. *ABC World News Tonight*, aired March 21, 1990.

4. Shirley Siluk, "Mulligan Victory Puts New Twist on Dem Challenge," *Park Ridge Advocate*, March 29, 2022.

5. *ABC World News Tonight*, aired March 21, 1990.

6. Burt Constable, "The Dollars and Sense in Pullen/Mulligan Fight," *Daily Herald*, September 5, 1991.

7. "Atheists Say Non-believers Were Difference in 55th Race," *Park Ridge Advocate*, April 5, 1990.

8. Shirley Siluk, "Atheists Knock 'Day of Prayer for Rain,'" *Park Ridge Advocate*, July 7, 1988.

9. Barbara Brotman, "Abortion Rights Activists Cheering Pullen Defeat," *Chicago Tribune*, March 22, 1990.

10. Tim Schmitz, interview with author, October 12, 2021.

11. Penny Pullen, interview by Mark DePue, session 2, April 22, 2020, Legislators Project, Abraham Lincoln Presidential Library and Museum, Springfield, IL.

12. Cal Skinner, "Memories of Top Election Law Attorney Mike Lavelle," *McHenry County Blog*, December 24, 2009.

13. Ibid.

14. Pullen, interview, session 2.

15. Gary Gale, interviews with author, August 4 and August 11, 2021.

16. Penny Pullen, interview by Mark DePue, session 3, April 29, 2020, Legislators Project, Abraham Lincoln Presidential Library and Museum, Springfield, IL.

17. Pat Milhizer, "Odelson Considered a 'Dean of Election Lawyers,'" *Chicago Daily Law Bulletin*, May 11, 2011.

18. Dave McKinney, "Coin Toss Today for 55th House Seat," *Daily Herald*, July 18, 1990.

19. Laura Janota, "Both Sides Declare Victory at Mulligan-Pullen Primary Trial," *Daily Herald*, June 22, 1990.

20. "Lawmaker Sues to Overturn Loss," *Southern Illinoisan* (AP), June 22, 1990.

21. Shirley Siluk, "Pullen, Mulligan Court Fight Nears Settlement," *Park Ridge Advocate*, June 28, 1990.

22. "Penny Pullen Campaign News," July 5, 1990, Calvin L. Skinner Jr. Papers, Northern Illinois University Regional History Center, DeKalb, IL.

23. Shirley Siluk, "Pullen Off to Court over Results," *Park Ridge Advocate*, April 19, 1990.

24. Shirley Siluk, "Mulligan Wins Race," *Park Ridge Advocate*, July 19, 1990.

25. Steve Bertrand, interview with Burt Odelson, *WGN News Radio*, aired October 29, 2020.

26. Francis Barth, interview with author, April 1, 2022.

Chapter 10. Heads or Tails

1. John McCormick, "Theresa Petrone 1923–2006," *Chicago Tribune*, December 6, 2006.

2. Mary A. Johnson, "It's Tails: Mulligan Wins Bid for Now," *Chicago Sun-Times*, July 19, 1990.

3. Shirley Siluk, "Mulligan Wins Race," *Park Ridge Advocate*, July 19, 1990.

4. Penny Pullen, interview by Mark DePue, session 3, April 29, 2020, Legislators Project, Abraham Lincoln Presidential Library and Museum, Springfield, IL.

5. Dave Urbanek, "Confident Pullen Ready for Primary Recount," *Daily Herald*, April 4, 1990.

6. Pullen, interview, session 3.

7. *Pullen v. Mulligan*, 138 Ill.2d 21 (1990), audio provided by the Illinois Supreme Court.

8. Francis Barth, interview with author, April 1, 2022.

9. *Pullen v. Mulligan*.

Chapter 11. Rematch

1. Letter from Penny Pullen, September 21, 1990, Calvin L. Skinner Jr. Papers, Northern Illinois University Regional History Center, DeKalb, IL.

2. Shirley Siluk, "Mucci Reveals His Campaign Platform," *Park Ridge Advocate*, June 14, 1990.

3. "Pullen Wins Despite Strong Vote for Mucci," *Park Ridge Advocate*, November 8, 1990.

4. 85th Illinois General Assembly, House Transcript, January 14, 1987.

5. 86th Illinois General Assembly, House Transcript, November 13, 1990.

6. "Penny Pullen Campaign News," April 1990, Calvin L. Skinner Jr. Papers, Northern Illinois University Regional History Center, DeKalb, IL.

7. Ray Long and Charles Wheeler III, "Pullen Wins It by 6 Ballots," *Chicago Sun-Times*, September 1, 1990.

8. Mary Ann Irvine, interview with author, September 1, 2021.

9. Bill Grady, Merrill Goozner, and John O'Brien, "Official Discord in Women's Bar," *Chicago Tribune*, August 14, 1990.

10. Burt Odelson, interview with author, September 1, 2022.

11. Jeanne Cummings and Chad Terhune, "Chad Enough? Dimpled Bits of Paper May Now Hold Key to Who Is President—But Partially Marked Ballots Have a Clouded History in Other Close Elections—Court Says Recounts Count," *Wall Street Journal*, November 22, 2000.

12. Elizabeth Owens, "GOP Remap Splits City District," *Park Ridge Advocate*, October 3, 1991.

13. "Column: Sneed," *Chicago Sun-Times*, May 22, 1991.

14. Debra Rowland, "Abortion Demonstrations Send 'Peaceful' Message," *Chicago Tribune*, May 20, 1991.

Chapter 12. Talk of the Town

1. "Talk of the Town," *Park Ridge Times Herald*, September 11, 18, and 25, 1991.
2. Sarah Craig, "Anti-Gay Lawmaker Penny Pullen Defeated," *Windy City Times*, March 29, 1990.
3. "Talk of the Town," *Park Ridge Times Herald*, September 11, 18, and 25, 1991.
4. Susan Kuczka, "Fiery Pullen-Mulligan Battle Rekindles," *Chicago Tribune*, February 26, 1992.
5. Rex Wockner, "Gays' Arch Foe Pullen Defeated," *Outlines*, April 1992.
6. Harlen Fleming, email correspondence with author.
7. "Talk of the Town," *Park Ridge Times Herald*, September 11, 18, and 25, 1991.
8. Ibid.
9. Matt Bonaguidi, interview with author, October 6, 2021.
10. "Reelection Rate Over the Years," *Open Secrets*, accessed December 21, 2022, https://www.opensecrets.org/elections-overview/reelection-rates.
11. Letter from Phyllis Schlafly, February 14, 1992, Calvin L. Skinner Jr. Papers, Northern Illinois University Regional History Center, DeKalb, IL.
12. Kuczka, "Fiery Pullen-Mulligan Battle Rekindles."
13. "Polish Guy in Chicago Changes His Name to Shannon O'Malley and Gets Elected Judge," *Irish Central*, November 8, 2018.
14. Nancy Keraminas, "55th Candidates Battle at Forum," *Park Ridge Times Herald*, March 4, 1992.
15. Doris Folkl, "State Candidates Scrap for Maine GOP Support," *Park Ridge Advocate*, January 16, 1992.
16. Ibid.
17. "Pullen's Area Office Rocked," *Des Plaines Journal*, September 4, 1991.
18. Bonaguidi, interview.
19. Susan Juczka and Joseph Kirby, "Candidates Place Hopes with 'Undecided,'" *Chicago Tribune*, March 17, 1992.

Chapter 13. Goldwater Girls

1. Flynn McRoberts, "Clinton's Wife a Hit Back Home," *Chicago Tribune*, March 12, 1992.
2. Joyce Milton, *The First Partner* (New York: Harper Paperbacks, 1999).
3. David Awbrey, "Penny Pullen Works Way Up the Conservative Ladder," *Herald and Review* (Decatur, IL), February 25, 1979.
4. Edward Klein, *The Truth About Hillary* (New York: Sentinel, 2005), 56–57.
5. Hillary Clinton, *Living History* (New York: Simon & Schuster, 2004), 24.
6. Christopher Anderson, *Bill and Hillary: The Marriage* (New York: William Morrow, 1999), 93.
7. Tom McNamee, "Ad Pressure Keeps Dixon from Voters," *Chicago Sun-Times*, March 14, 1992.
8. Mary Ann Irvine, interview with author, September 1, 2021.

9. "Political Pundit Asks for Probe of Mulligan $$," *Des Plaines Journal*, February 28, 1992.

10. Susan Kuczka, "Abstinence Group Finds Tie to Pullen Pays," *Chicago Tribune*, March 4, 1992.

11. "Political Briefing," *Chicago Sun-Times*, September 27, 1991.

12. Doris Folkl, "Pullen Rejects Ethics Charge," *Park Ridge Advocate*, March 5, 1992.

13. Rick Pearson and Robert Vitale, "Legislative Remap Finds Pullen among Victims," *Chicago Tribune*, March 18, 1992.

14. Dan Mihalopoulos, "Justices Eye 1990 Illinois Ruling Recount Reversed Outcome of Race," *Chicago Tribune*, November 21, 2000.

15. Terry Pryzbylski, "Mulligan People Showed Anything but Class Tuesday," *Des Plaines Journal*, March 25, 1992.

16. "The 90's Election Specials Raw: Clintons at Maine South High School #2," *Mediaburn.org*, https://mediaburn.org/video/the-90s-election-specials-raw-clintons-at-maine-south-high-school-2/.

17. "The 90's Election Specials Raw: Channel 7 News Primary Election Night," *Mediaburn.org*, https://mediaburn.org/video/the-90s-election-specials-raw-channel-7-news-primary-election-night/.

18. Terry Cosgrove, interview with author, August 23, 2021.

19. Penny Pullen, interview by Mark DePue, session 3, April 29, 2020, Legislators Project, Abraham Lincoln Presidential Library and Museum, Springfield, IL.

20. "The 90's Election Specials Raw: Channel 7 News Primary Election Night."

21. Letter from Penny Pullen, March 24, 1992, Calvin L. Skinner, Jr. Papers, Northern Illinois University Regional History Center, DeKalb, IL.

22. Susan Kuczka, "GOP Loses Ground in Northwest," *Chicago Tribune*, March 22, 1992.

Epilogue

1. Mary Ann Irvine, interview with author, September 1, 2021.

2. Ibid.

3. Aaron Chambers, "Blagojevich Has Put Off Friends and Foes," *CantonRep.com*, November 5, 2007.

4. "Nick Skala Questioned by Rosemary Mulligan," Illinois Media Progressives, Internet Archives, August 12, 2009, https://archive.org/details/HCAI-RM-NS.

5. Colleen Mastony, "Mulligan, Jones Not Far Apart on Issues," *Chicago Tribune*, October 23, 2002.

6. Jill Rosen, "Americans Don't Know Much about State Government, Survey Finds," *Hub* (Johns Hopkins University newsletter), December 14, 2018.

Index